Christian Life Center
1310 Portage Rd.
Kalamazoo, Mi 49001
344-7135

Successfully Single

Yvonne G. Baker

ACCENT BOOKS
Denver. CO 80215

ACCENT BOOKS

A division of Accent Publications, Inc.
12100 West Sixth Avenue
P.O. Box 15337
Denver, Colorado 80215

Library of Congress Catalog Card Number 85-070989

ISBN 0-89636-163-2

Dedicated to

Sandi, Togi, Mary and Chris—
wonderful, successful single women

ACKNOWLEDGMENTS

Special thanks to all the women who shared their lives, experiences and questions with me as I wrote this book. Though names and some identifying circumstances have been changed in the book to protect privacy, without them the book could not have been written.

In addition to the many people I spoke with, this book is the result of a multitude of written excerpts found in newspaper articles, magazines and books. Though I have tried to accurately quote all my sources, I realize I have pieced together in my memory many things I have studied over the past few years. I take responsibility for their final form, but I acknowledge that many ideas did not begin with me.

Special thanks also to all the writers like Sylvia Porter who teach us how to organize and control our lives. One special author I would like to acknowledge is Mimi Brien. Her book, *Moneywise*, was the first truly helpful book I read as a newly divorced and very afraid woman. Not only does her book contain excellent, practical advice, but her hope and positive attitude have been an inspiration to me.

My most important source also needs to be acknowledged. It is God's Word, the Bible. The practical advice in this book comes from many sources. But what I have used, I have tried to make sure was in accordance with God's Word. For the single life—or any life—I believe the Bible is the only source of truth, hope and counsel for truly successful living.

All quotes from the Bible, unless otherwise noted, are from the *New International Version*, published by The International Bible Society, 1973, 1978.

CONTENTS

CONTENTS

Introduction

It was the mouse that finally devastated me.

I'd seen evidence of him for weeks: in my kitchen, behind books on shelves, everywhere. At first I ignored him and just hoped he'd go away. He didn't.

I bought a mousetrap. But mousetraps don't come with instructions on how to set them. Several bruised fingers later I had my mother show me how. Then I realized that if I caught it, I didn't know what to do with a dead mouse. Worse yet, what if he was all bloody and half alive? I threw away the traps.

The mouse got braver. One night he ran across the couch. I screamed and huddled against the cushions. Then the mouse came out from behind the bookcase and just sat there looking at me. I burst into tears. He'd won. My husband had always taken care of mousetraps and now I had no husband. I felt stupid and childish, incompetent and scared to death.

That mouse symbolized the chaos of my current life. During the 13 years of my married life, I had concentrated on things like making good meals and a comfortable home. I had learned how to entertain friends, to practice love and to exercise hospitality. I grew flowers and relationships. I worked some, but the focus of my life was my home and my church. I loved it that way. To be dependent, to let someone else take care of taxes and house payments and those sorts of things was what I thought I was supposed to do. Suddenly that life was all gone and I found my responsibilities totally alien.

Suddenly, overwhelmingly, I realized that I didn't know how to do anything practical.

Insurance, cars and mortgages cluttered my befuddled senses. It was a wilderness without a map. Through all my female life, my best learned skills were careful relational ones and now they were useless.

I didn't know where to begin.

11

"But seek ye first the kingdom of God, and his righteousness; and all these things shall be added unto you."
                                    Matthew 6:33, KJV

1

BEGINNING

Maybe you are like me.

Maybe you're a woman alone.

Maybe you are divorced. Years of counseling, trying, crying and resolving didn't work and you feel your life is destroyed.

Maybe you are a widow. Perhaps you were looking forward to a long retirement with your husband. Then one morning he didn't come in from getting the mail, and you found him on the sidewalk dead of a heart attack.

Maybe you decided you had to grow up. You moved out of your parents' home and into your own apartment or an unfamiliar city.

Maybe the man in your life just walked out one day. Or maybe he abused you or your children and you walked out. Maybe you just realized your "trial separation" has become permanent.

Maybe nothing traumatic happened. Yet you find yourself by yourself. You are alone.

NOW WHAT?

Maybe you cry. Maybe you lock the door against mounting bills, credit reminders and just panic.

As a Christian you pray. You read your Bible. That comforts your soul and gives you peace, but you know you still have a lot of decisions to make.

Questions such as these flood your life:

Where will I find a place to live? How will I pay the rent or make the house payments? Should I find a roommate?

What do I do about insurance for me, for the car? What is renter's insurance?

How can I get a job that will support my kids and me?

How can I get credit? Or cash checks? Or get a loan?

What happens if the car breaks down?

What about a will?

The list goes on and on, filled with the sometimes terrifying trivia of daily life.

Unfortunately, Christian women are especially trauma-tized at a time of sudden—sometimes unwanted—independence. We learn how to be good wives and mothers. We are taught to be submissive and cheerful, dependent and caring. All this is wonderful but not necessarily pertinent to a single woman's life. Most churches would never think of offering a workshop for women on buying their own insurance and doing car maintenance. Credit in your own name and sound investments are not exactly women's Bible study topics.

Many genuinely caring peers often turn away or remain blissfully unaware of difficult times. A single mother's problems can be too overwhelming. A widow's sorrow can seem to be a burden if she mourns too long. A never married adult can be too threatening to the established order of things.

Understanding that other people may avoid you because they don't know what to do doesn't help when you're alone. You don't know what to do either.

There are all sorts of popular self-help books which show a woman how to recognize her "crazy time" and her "Cinderella complex." This reading can be useful, but as Kendra, a recently divorced woman, said, "After awhile I got sick of all the emotionally helpful stuff—I still didn't know how to buy car insurance, or get a credit card in my name." Emotions do need evaluation, rearranging and, periodically, some healing. But emotions aside, the single woman faces a deluge of realities.

BASIC NEEDS

The basic physical needs such as shelter, food, and safety are as important to God as the needs for love and self-esteem. You may be unemployed, overdrawn at the bank or depressed with a four week old cold. But God gives wisdom to take care of the practical things in life. He cares about your bank balance as well as the cold. And, it's amazing how much better you feel about yourself, God, and life in general once the practical aspects of life are tackled with His wisdom.

One psychologist describes the basic needs of human beings as fitting into two primary areas. He says that first of all we need, "maximum human accessibility—in other words—we need people." The second thing we need is "a minimum nurturing environment—housing, income, insurance, etc.,—the practical concerns of life."

OTHER PEOPLE CARE ABOUT YOU, TOO

We were left on this earth in a body to be there for one another, to help and build one another up. That's the reason for this book. As a woman who has struggled and is struggling with the concerns discussed, I've learned a lot. I want to share it with you. Don't try to be an island. We are social by nature. Get a friend or relative to help you with certain matters, get advice from experts, that sort of thing. Just because you are without a spouse doesn't mean you don't need people in your life. Be a friend. Look for and ask God for people to fill your life with love and support. That is one of the most important ingredients for a successfully single life.

Think of this book as a tool box. Step by step it lights the way through the practical areas of life that every single woman needs in order to live successfully. Each chapter will focus on one specific aspect of life: jobs, insurance, housing, family relationships, money, legal matters, food and fitness, psychological helps, social life, personal appearance, security and many other areas. Each chapter gives specific ideas and instruction, shared experiences of other women in these situations, and suggestions for additional resources and readings. In the areas where it makes a difference, there will be specific advice for different situations: divorced, widowed, separated or just starting out on your own.

Like my friend Amy, you can decide to approach life as a responsible, adult woman. She realized she had a lot to learn, but she didn't deny her need to learn. She realized that building a successful life required some tools she may not have had a chance to develop yet, but she decided that she was going to learn to use them.

Amy is a Christian, but that didn't make her immune to problems. God was there with all His resources and wisdom, but the choice of how to use them, belonged solely to her.

I hope you, too, choose Amy's way. I hope you take a deep breath and calmly decide that you are going to make your life a work of art. Maybe not a painting, carefully brushed onto a smooth canvas, but a mosaic, a masterpiece formed by small pieces, and put together very carefully until at last its beauty is evident to all.

You won't be alone. No matter how lonely you may feel at times, remember the Lord has promised never to leave you or to forsake you. When you get depressed or overwhelmed with all you have to do, think about the following passage:

"Do not be afraid; you will not suffer shame.
Do not fear disgrace; you will not be humiliated.
You will forget the shame of your youth
and remember no more the reproach of your widowhood.
For your Maker is your husband—
The Lord Almighty is his name—
the Holy One of Israel is your Redeemer;
he is called the God of all the earth.
The Lord will call you back
as if you were a wife deserted and
distressed in spirit—
a wife who married young, only to be rejected," says your God.
"For a brief moment I abandoned you,
but with deep compassion I will
bring you back.
In a surge of anger
I hid my face from you for a
moment,
but with everlasting kindness
I will have compassion on you,"
says the Lord your Redeemer....
"Though the mountains be shaken
and the hills be removed,
yet my unfailing love for you will not
be shaken
nor my covenant of peace be removed,"
says the Lord, who has compassion
on you.
Isaiah 54:4-8,10

17

Because of space limitations, suggestions are given for additional reading if you want to pursue an area, such as investments, in more detail. At the same time, if you follow the advice in the practical areas of this book, you will be more organized and better prepared to control your life than 90 percent of the women in America, single or married.

HOW TO USE THIS BOOK

The topics are arranged in alphabetical order. Some sections are brief. Some, like the section on employment, are quite lengthy. There are also subsections that discuss some topics in more detail. Each section will also refer you to other sections if they apply.

You can read through the whole book or just the parts you need. Be patient as you learn more about the various areas in your life. It is easy to feel overwhelmed when you may feel like you need help in every area. Some women find it helpful to make a schedule or write down the order in which they intend to handle certain concerns. For example, one week you may choose to tackle auto insurance, the next week talk to the bank about credit cards in your own name. If you start to panic, you're probably attempting to do too much at one time. Your world won't completely collapse if you don't get everything figured out tomorrow, so don't be too hard on yourself.

The choice is yours. You can stay where you are, or you can make your time alone an exciting adventure. More than that, you can be *SUCCESSFULLY* SINGLE!

> *"Have I not commanded you? Be strong and courageous! Do not tremble or be dismayed, for the Lord your God is with you wherever you go."*
> Joshua 1:9 (NASB)

Additional Recommended Reading:

I Gave God Time by Ann Kiemel Anderson
Living and Loving the Single Life by Luci Swindoll
Wide My World, Narrow My Bed by Luci Swindoll

2

APPEARANCE

"Why look good?" Kathy wailed. "All I have is me. I don't have anybody to look good for."

Good question. From childhood on we've been taught to look nice for something or someone—get dressed up for church, do your hair for a date—if the someone or something isn't there, why bother?

The reason to bother is because the most important person in your life is worth it. That person is you. Remember that the standard for loving others is how we love ourselves (Mark 12:30,31). If we don't love and care for ourselves, we won't care for others or our work. If you see yourself as worthless, you will unconsciously sabotage everything you do. If you see yourself as being valuable to God and view your life with purpose, you'll reflect that also.

> *"You are precious and honored in my sight... I love you."*
>
> Isaiah 43:4

Precious, honored and loved by Almighty God. Let the outside of you reflect that reality!

LET'S GET PRACTICAL

"My wardrobe is a mess!" said Jenny, "I go shopping if I feel like it, and I buy what looks good at the time. When I get home, half the time I don't like it and it doesn't go with anything else I have. I have lots of clothes, but so often there is nothing I want to wear."

Her problem with clothes is common, but easy to solve with a little planning and foresight.

Before you get into the specifics of wardrobe renovation, evaluate your lifestyle. As a writer I work at home. And even though it is important to me to shower, put on my makeup and wear clean clothes, I don't need the type of wardrobe I would if I worked in an office.

If you are going back to or starting work, your wardrobe needs will be completely different. At work your appearance must reflect a professional image. Don't look like the poor housewife or the casually dressed mother on the job. You have to dress the part to get the part. One of the best ways of learning what constitutes a professional image is to go to meetings of women in the professional field of your interest and see what they are wearing. You can also look through some of the magazines for professional women. Looking professional does not mean dressing expensively. You can get a nice suit on sale for what some of the designer jeans cost today.

After you have decided what type of clothes your work and lifestyle require, consider the following two concepts I have found extremely useful. The first has to do with colors and the second with how you coordinate your clothes.

HAVE YOUR COLORS DONE

Terri showed me her little card with swatches of colored fabric arranged on it. "These are my colors," she

22

said. "I can take this chart shopping and it shows me what I look best in. It keeps me from making expensive mistakes by buying things I don't really look good in and won't wear."

I thought that was the dumbest thing I ever heard—when she first told me about it. Then a friend had my colors done for me as a gift. After trying a few of the principles I learned from that session, I quickly changed my mind.

The whole theory in all its various forms revolves around the basic idea that your skin has either blue or yellow undertones, which is why you look good in some colors and awful in others. These two types of coloring are then divided into two other areas and in most schemes the four categories are named after the seasons. A color consultant can help you find out what season you are by holding up various pieces of colored fabric next to your skin. It is truly amazing the difference various colors can make in your appearance. You can also get a very good idea of your skin type without a color consultant. Look at one of the books on color theory. *Color Me Beautiful* is one of them, but there are numerous others that are similar. Once you have decided what season you fit into, you have a certain group of colors that look good on you. This basic principle can guide you in your wardrobe and makeup color selection.

This is how it worked for me. I am an autumn. That means I look good in fall colors: browns, tans, yellows, plus accents like salmon and aqua. I look awful in white, black, pink and other primary and pastel colors. Once I found that out, I realized why I could never find a white blouse I liked or a pink lipstick that looked good on me. Several of my friends and I did this at the same time and what didn't work for us, we traded with each other. Now my shopping and wardrobe coordination is so much simpler. Almost everything in my closet goes with all my other things. My accessories match and I like what I wear much more than I ever did before.

Once I did my colors, I then discovered another very useful wardrobe system.

CAPSULE DRESSING

This system was called "mix and match" when I was in high school; "dressing with coordinates" when I was in college. Now it's called "capsule dressing." But whatever the name, it is a timeless and sensible way to dress. All it means is that you buy clothes that you can wear interchangeably.

The book, *Working Wardrobe*, by Janet Wallach (Warner Books, 1981), is an excellent book explaining the whole concept. You first pick two colors. (Here is where the color background comes in. You, of course, pick two of your best colors.) For example, red and black, which is perfect if you are a winter. Then you purchase or use from your existing wardrobe 12 pieces of clothing consisting of items such as a black jacket and black skirt, white blouse, red sweater and shirtdress, etc. By combining the various pieces, in the two coordinating colors plus white, you can make 48 different looks. You can vary your system depending upon your lifestyle and budget, but it gives you a plan that works in a simple and sensible way.

MAKE IT PRACTICAL

With an idea of what your best colors are and a rough plan of the sort of interchangeable capsule or wardrobe looks you would like, below are tips for putting these ideas into practice.

1) Know exactly what you have in your wardrobe now

Take everything out of your closet. See what goes with what, what you look good in and what you don't. What are your colors, what aren't. What fits into your lifestyle *now*—not what you wish it would be—and what doesn't. Be realistic. I saved a pair of jeans I was able to pour myself into when I was in college for years thinking someday they would fit again. I finally had to face the fact that I would have to cut off one leg to weigh what I did then—so out went the jeans.

2) Plan for changes

You can't change everything overnight, but you will accomplish your goals by following some of these tips step by step.

★ Give away, sell or trade what you don't look good in and never wear anymore.

★ Learn to shop wisely and well. This means getting the most for your money. Learn to shop at some of the stores that sell name brand clothing for less. Know when sales are happening. Buy quality, classic clothes that last.

★ Remember: God cares about every detail of your life. I always pray before shopping: specifically for what I am looking for, and for wisdom. A few winters ago I needed a winter coat and I didn't have much money. I prayed for one before going to Denver to shop. I'd just had my colors figured out and I added a P.S. to my prayers that I would like the coat to be in brown. They just happened to have a big sale on winter coats up there that day and I found a perfect 100% wool coat for $30.00. It was a warm, soft, chocolate brown.

Additional Recommended Reading:

Color Me Beautiful by Carol Johnson
Dress With Style by Joanne Wallace

*"Be anxious for nothing, but in every-
thing by prayer and supplication with
thanksgiving let your requests be made
known to God."*

Philippians 4:6, NASB

3

AUTOMOBILES

If you are recently singled, you've probably discovered
that in the usual marriage, women cook and men work on
cars. When a marriage ends a man can go to a fast food
outlet and with little effort on his part get something to
eat.

It isn't that easy to take care of a car. There are a lot of
things a single woman has to consider. If you've never
been married, a father, brother or male friend may have
been helping, but there are still some things easier to
ignore than others. Insurance, for example, may be
essential, but you aren't reminded every day that your
insurance will be due in six months. And a car is almost
omnipresent. There it sits, needing gas and oil and
making funny noises. You can't do without a car. You
have to have it to get groceries, to go to work or to take
the kids various places.

A car also costs a lot to buy and keep. Next to a house,
it is the most expensive purchase you will make. Sylvia
Porter states that we spend 13-15 cents out of every

dollar to own and operate our cars. If you purchased a car in 1982 and keep it for 12 years, at the end of that time you will have spent over $32,000 on it. With these statistics in mind, the importance of decisions made concerning a car is obvious.

There are two primary areas of concern with cars. First is getting the proper car and second is maintaining it. Let's consider them in that order.

DECIDING WHAT CAR TO BUY

Maybe your old car just died. Maybe your husband got the car and you got the house in a divorce settlement. Maybe your job requires a different kind of car. Whatever the reason, you find yourself looking for another car. How do you decide what to get? Do you get a new or used car?

There are a number of factors to consider when looking for any car. Take time to carefully think through each of the areas below before deciding which one to buy.

LIFESTYLE AND PERSONAL NEEDS: My friend Jackie is a real estate agent. She needs a nice car in which to take clients around and one that is roomy enough for her several children. Joyce is a saleswoman. She doesn't take clients in her car, but she needs a reliable automobile that gets good gas mileage and is comfortable since she spends many hours in it. I write at home and have a 1975 Honda with 150,000 miles on it. Each of our car needs, based on our individual lifestyles, is drastically different. It would be as foolish for me to drive the car Jackie does as it would be for her to show people around in my little, ten-year-old Honda.

BUDGET: Once you know the kind of car you need, there are still a lot of choices to make. If you need a nice car, there are nice Chevrolets and nice Mercedeses; your budget will help you to realistically choose which is best for you. All of the areas below should be considered as you evaluate your car budget.

DEPRECIATION: Depreciation means how much a car decreases in value as it gets older. It is often forgotten when considering a car purchase, but depreciation is one of the largest automotive costs. On the average, a new car loses 30 percent of its value the first year, 18 percent the second year, 13 percent the third year, the fourth year 9 percent, the fifth year 3-5 percent and after that only 1 or 2 percent per year. What this means, in practical terms to you, is that you pay a lot for a brand new car and lose a lot on a car that you trade in after only a couple of years.

If you keep a car for about 10 years, the depreciation costs will average out. Or, you can consider purchasing a used car. This will be discussed in more detail later. Used cars don't just mean old junkers.

MAINTENANCE AND OTHER COSTS: This varies tremendously with each car. A small foreign sports car can be a lot of fun to drive, but to have engine work done at a specialized repair shop and to have custom parts serviced can be a nightmare. A large, older car can cost you a fortune in tires as well as frequent repairs.

To find out what various car repair costs average, consult *Consumer Reports*, a magazine that virtually every library has. There are special issues devoted to cars and you may find some of the results surprising.

While on the subject of varying car costs, don't forget to figure expenses for gas mileage, taxes, and car insurance. These can vary tremendously between cars.

One final cost to consider is the resale value. This is especially important if you plan to trade cars regularly. Your bank or car dealer will have a Blue Book which gives car values for cars up to seven years of age. My Honda, which I bought used, actually went up in value for the first couple of years I had it. This was at a time when the gas shortage was just beginning and its great gas mileage was a valuable asset.

KEEP IN MIND: Cars are tremendously important in our lives and budgets, but when you are deciding which car to purchase, don't forget they are only an intricately manufactured piece of metal.

One woman recently told me a story about her car that broke my heart. "I decided I needed a sporty, expensive car to fit into my new image when I was first divorced," she told me. She sighed and continued. "The car cost a lot. So did insurance and other things. Eventually I had to take an evening job to pay for it. I temporarily turned over the custody of my son to his father who soon remarried. His new wife stayed home and raised Timmy. In a year, I was making enough to quit the evening job and I wanted Timmy back. But he hardly recognized me. Jean is his mother now and I get him one weekend a month."

NEW OR USED CAR?

After you've thought through some of the general areas above, you need to decide whether you will get a new car or a used car. There are a number of pros and cons to consider for both choices.

USED CARS: I have personally had very good luck with used cars. For all of my adult life I have purchased used cars that were each under three years old when I got them. Several of them were almost new when I purchased them, and they were all subsequently driven over a hundred thousand miles. I think my little Honda will make it to two hundred thousand. Since finances are usually of concern to single women, used cars should be seriously considered because of their cheaper price. Good luck with used cars, however, is not just based on chance. It is founded on careful groundwork before you purchase the car. Be sure to follow the tips below:

★ Get recommendations from other single women and married friends as to good used car dealers. In one of the singles' Sunday School classes in my town, there is a man who owns a used car lot. He specializes in helping single women find cars which are right for them. Other dealers have been around a long time and have good reputations. Try to find them through recommendations from others who have bought used cars or call your local Better Business Bureau to check out a dealer's reputation.

★ Remember that when a dealer offers a used car for sale "as is," it means he is not making any promises that the car is in good shape or that he will repair it if something goes wrong. And, whether stated or not, that is always the condition under which you purchase a car from a private party through the newspaper.

★ Look at the car in the daylight, not in the dark after work. It's amazing how much more you can see.

★ Be sure to take the car for a test drive. At that time get permission to take it to a diagnostic center or your garage and have the engine and major parts checked. If a long list comes back of things wrong with the car, ask the mechanic to explain them to you. I once got a huge list on a car I had checked out at a diagnostic center, but all of the items were very small things such as worn out hoses. I purchased the car and it served me well for quite a few years. On the other hand, one major item, like a cracked block in the engine, definitely means you should not purchase the car.

★ If you have a friend who knows a lot about cars and he or she is willing, have them come along with you for all of this. A second opinion on any major purchase is always useful.

★ If you are shy about negotiating on the price of a used car, pretend you are somebody else; be brave and do it. The salesman doesn't expect you to pay the first price asked. By all means talk to your bank, too, if you are going to have your car financed. Find out all of the loan costs and the Blue Book (also known as the Kelly Auto Market Report) value of the car, so you know what is realistic to spend. Then add or deduct for hard wear or low mileage or whatever. Don't forget to add tire replacement costs if the tires are excessively worn. Don't feel pressured to agree to a car sale before you think through these things. Of course, all of this takes time, but careful shopping for a used car can save you thousands of dollars.

NEW CARS: If you decide on a new car, there are still quite a few factors to consider. Buying a new car does not guarantee that you are purchasing a car without problems.

The price of new cars can vary tremendously. I recently went to look at new cars and was amazed to discover that some models were almost double the price of others. Some were year end models, some had all the extras, some were very simple, but all were new cars.

Decide what options you want before you go shopping and are tempted. Options can increase the price of a car by up to 50 percent. When you sit down with a dealer to talk about the price of a car, be sure all costs including taxes, license fees, delivery prices, final car preparations, any options and miscellaneous costs are figured in. Don't hesitate to take someone more knowledgeable with you if that will make you more comfortable.

Just because you are at a new car dealership, don't assume the car is mechanically perfect. Be sure to test drive it. New cars can have lots of mechanical problems and if you are buying a car in stock, it doesn't hurt to have your mechanic check out that particular vehicle.

Don't be afraid to bargain with new cars either. A few minutes of bravery can be worth hundreds of dollars to you.

Finally on a new car, do not accept delivery until all repairs have been done. It's easy for the dealer to promise all sorts of things for the future, but once he has your money, he might not be as eager to take care of things as he was when he was selling you the car. Be sure, too, you understand your warranty completely before you take the car. Some very simple repairs or the neglect of certain items can needlessly invalidate a warranty.

HOW TO PAY FOR THE CAR YOU SELECTED— FINANCING TIPS

"I thought a car dealership was the only place I could finance my car," said Jeanie. "I didn't realize that you could shop for a car loan just like anything else."

Not only can you shop for a car loan, but there are a number of places to try. Two out of every three people who purchase a car finance it. Looking for the right car loan is almost as important as finding the right car.

First of all, ask the dealer what sort of loan he will provide. Get all the details down in writing and use it for a comparison. Next, go to the bank where you have your checking and savings account. Ask what sort of a loan package they can provide. Finally, if you are a member of a credit union, be sure to ask them. Sometimes they provide especially good deals to members.

When you arrange for financing on a car, make the largest down payment possible and arrange the loan for the shortest amount of time. This will keep the cost of the loan down.

When you set up the loan, be sure you understand all of the details of the financing. This means knowing what the total cost of the loan will be: the amount you borrow, the interest charges over the life of the loan and the late charge. Also, consider taking out credit life insurance and a disability policy on the loan. The credit life insurance means the loan will be paid off in the event of your death. A disability policy will make the payments if you are unable to make them because of accident or illness.

HOW TO TAKE CARE OF A CAR NOW THAT YOU'VE GOT IT

"Cars are a pain!" Amy was almost yelling as she related to me all the money she had spent on car repairs in the last year. I had to agree with her as I picked up my car from the garage for the third time in a month.

To minimize the trouble and repair bills that come with car ownership, below are a number of hints on preventive car care along with some tips on car safety:

★ Always make sure you have enough gas in your car. It sounds too simple to mention, but if you are used to someone else filling the tank, being stranded alone at night on a dark street is a bad time to realize that it's your job now.

★ Check the oil frequently, especially on older cars. I have to add oil every time I get gas. That is excessive, but it keeps my car running until I can afford to have the repairs made. The mechanic I go to recommends that you not use cheap generic oil. But to save money, go to a discount store and buy good oil by the case. It's equally important, I was told, to have your oil changed at the proper intervals for your car.

★ Make sure your tires have the right amount of air and that you rotate them properly. I had to buy new tires the first year I was alone because I didn't know that. I have a car that has front wheel drive and I completely wore out the front pair of radial tires. Also, be sure to keep your spare tire full of air and in good repair.

★ Periodically go to a full service gas station and have them check the gas, oil and air filters, and the water level in your battery if it is not a maintenance free one. Antifreeze is important also as Joyce found out when she moved to Colorado from Texas. We spent one day trying to unfreeze her engine with my little portable heater when an early Colorado snow fell on her warm weather radiator.

★ When you go in for specific repairs, ask the mechanic to check for other potential problems. If the shop is reputable, they won't tell you things are wrong when they aren't, and spotting a potential problem before it becomes a major one is very important. When I had a flat tire changed recently, the mechanic warned me my brakes were wearing. The difference between new linings and a new set of brake drums, if the linings had worn through, was quite significant.

★ Be sure to have funny noises checked out, especially if they are loud and clanging and come from under the hood. Things rarely get better by themselves. I have been known to pray for healing for my little car. But when I was honest with myself, my prayer has more often reflected laziness rather than faith on my part.

★ Always have your car checked over before you go on a long trip. You don't want to have major repairs done on the road at a small shop you know nothing about. Even if they are honest, they may not have the parts or equipment or knowledge to do a proper job.

★ One of the best things a single woman can do for herself is to belong to an auto club. The Automobile Association of America (AAA) is probably the best known, but several other companies are also available. An auto club provides towing, car starts and tire changes. My auto club membership provides an excellent publication that has taught me a lot about cars, provides discounts on car items and repairs, and tells me where I can take classes on car information. When my car broke down and nothing could start it, instead of panicking or trying to call friends to see who had a chain to tow it, I called my auto club number, ate an ice cream cone and when they arrived, was towed for free to my garage.

Major repairs will be discussed below, but for little emergencies and problems, it doesn't hurt to have the following items in your car: a spare tire and a jack that works, jumper cables, all weather coolant, a simple tool kit with pliers and screwdrivers, duct tape for leaks in hoses, paper towels for wiping off windows and the oil reservoir dip stick, windshield cleaner, premoistened towelettes, and, if you live in a cold climate, sand, a small shovel and chains for really severe driving conditions. A flashlight, flares and a simple first aid kit should complete the collection.

Also, keep in your car a record of all repairs, purchases, oil changes and tune ups so you know what to tell the mechanic when you take it in to the garage. It's also a good idea to keep in your car the owner's manual for your model if you have it, your warranty, insurance information (including your agent's phone number), and the telephone number of your auto club or a towing service. The car registration is required by law to be in your car at all times, but do not keep the title to your car in it. That should always be kept in a safe place where it cannot be lost or stolen.

WHEN SOMETHING GOES WRONG

I used to think I was very easy on my car. All I did was stop and go driving around town. I was quite surprised to learn in a recent AAA magazine that I am considered a "severe service driver." I found out that this kind of constant in-town driving is the most difficult on a car. The article went on to say that anyone doing this sort of driving should be especially careful to observe the owner's manual maintenance recommendations. To take care of these things, it was essential to find a good mechanic.

"Be careful, they'll tell a woman anything."

"They'll overcharge you. They do that to women."

"The car sometimes comes out of the garage in worse shape than it went in."

On and on I heard the warnings and I was terrified. Sort of like being afraid to go to the dentist, I just avoided the subject of car repair until my car started a high squealing noise that wouldn't quit.

Discovering a good mechanic is pure joy. The best way is through recommendations from others who know cars or from other women. That's how I found an independent Honda garage. They keep records on each car, just like a doctor does on a patient. I can call them to discuss problems before taking the car in, and they will give me preliminary advice over the phone.

They explain things in a language I can understand. I get an estimate before any work is done, and often, the final total is below the estimate. The garage is clean, well organized and has modern equipment. Best of all, my little Honda is running well.

There are a number of additional factors to consider when thinking about car care.

It has been fashionable lately for car care classes to be offered for women. I think these are an excellent idea, but NOT so you can learn to work on your own car. If you take a car care class, you will learn the proper names and descriptions of car parts. With this information, you can better describe a problem and take better preventative care of your car. One class and one general manual will not make you a mechanic. A good mechanic has had years of very specialized training and uses extremely expensive equipment. You can not only mess up a "simple" repair, but parts can fall into odd places and the job can quickly become very complex and expensive.

When you have found a garage you want to deal with, be sure to treat them courteously. Call to make an appointment—a good garage is just as busy as a doctor's office. Get a written estimate of the work to be done. If they do not keep maintenance records, be sure you do. Let the mechanic know where to reach you by phone if you must leave your car there. Road test the car when you pick it up and return it immediately if there are still problems. Be sure to express your appreciation for a job well done.

WHEN ALL ELSE FAILS

Sometimes, no matter how hard you tried, how much you thought you checked things out and did the right thing, you can still have terrible problems with your car— whether one that is newly purchased or recently repaired. You are not alone. The Consumer Information Office in Washington D.C. gets more complaints about cars than any other item.

If you do have problems, first of all state your complaint to the dealer or garage responsible for the problem. Sometimes having the proper records and being asser- tive is enough. If it is not, try your local Better Business Bureau, or, if your city is large enough, the local Consumer Affairs Office. If the problem is still unsolved, there are two national organizations that can help. For cars still under warranty, call PROJECT AUTOLINE. For a car that is no longer under warranty contact AUTO CAP. Both groups have a variety of methods for solving disputes that range from negotiations between the consumer and a dealer representative to impartial, binding arbitration. Look in the Yellow Pages or call information for the local numbers.

Additional Recommended Reading:

Consumer Magazine issues that deal with cars
Chiltons: Repair and Tune Up Guide Chilton Book
  Company

"There hath no temptation taken you but such as is common to man: but God is faithful, who will not suffer you to be tempted above that ye are able; but will with the temptation also make a way to escape, that ye may be able to bear it."
I Corinthians 10:13, KJV

4

CHEMICAL DEPENDENCY

"Do you think my daughter is addicted?" Lisa asked me with tears in her eyes.

It was all I could do to keep from shouting at her. Her daughter was in a detention home for delinquent teenagers. She had been put there by the police who had caught her trying to sell drugs at her high school. This was the third time she had been caught and the principal had finally called the police.

"How can you be so blind? Yes! She's addicted." I wanted to say. Lisa had found her daughter passed out in her room and smelling of alcohol. She'd found drug related items in her daughter's coat. And now Cindy was in a detention center. But as I hugged Lisa, a single mother going through a divorce, I had to remind myself of an important thing I'd learned from counseling classes and classes on drug abuse—one of the primary reactions to any sort of chemical abuse is denial. Whether it is alcohol, drugs such as marijuana and cocaine or prescription drugs, everyone rationalizes that it can't be a problem for them or their children.

Why the denial? Fear. We are afraid. Afraid of exposure, afraid of the shame involved, afraid that nothing we can do will help anyway. There is only one refuge from this kind of fear: *"When I am afraid, I will trust in you. In God whose word I praise, in God I trust; I will not be afraid"* (Psalm 56:3,4).

God knows everything about us—all the ugly, shameful, hurtful things. He doesn't deny anything.

> *"O Lord, you have searched me and you know me. You know when I sit and when I rise; you perceive my thoughts from afar. You discern my going out and my lying down; you are familiar with all my ways .... Where can I go from your Spirit? Where can I flee from your presence?"*
>
> Psalm 139:1-3,7

And yet, even knowing all of this, He promises that He will not take His love away from us, nor will He break His promises to us (Psalm 89:33-34). This assurance that we are loved—no matter what—gives us the courage to face the problems of chemical dependency in ourselves or in those we love.

IT'S A FAMILY PROBLEM

"I realized," Lisa told me after her daughter entered a drug rehabilitation program, "that her problem has been a *family* problem. They told us that the rest of us were reacting to her in ways that are patterned and predictable and just as much of a problem as Cindy's drug dependency."

This realization that drug dependency involves all of the family is one of the most important concepts in understanding and treating chemical dependency. Even if the chemically dependent person receives help, some of the other family members, whose lives have also been deeply affected, can be ignored. This, in turn, can cause the addiction to return or cause problems for the other family members later in life. For example, a child of alcoholic parents may try to be perfect in order to avoid physical abuse. This child can grow up to be an unhappy perfectionist, never able to relax in a relationship because he is fearful that life will fall apart if he ever makes a mistake.

Or, like Lisa, they can deny that the addictive person in their family has a problem. Lisa made excuses for her daughter, saying she was ill when she was drunk or on drugs. Because of that, Cindy never had to face the consequences of her actions. It wasn't until Lisa admitted that Cindy had a problem that her daughter was able to enter a treatment program.

The important thing to realize is that chemical dependency is more than just abuse of a substance whether it is drugs or alcohol. Chemical dependency affects everyone associated with the dependent person and treatment must involve all concerned.

ALCOHOLISM

Acknowledging that alcoholism is a disease does not relieve a person who is an alcoholic of responsibility for his actions. Alcohol affects some people much more strongly than others. You cannot help your particular response, but you can decide what to do about it.

Failure to deal with alcoholism is what the Bible defines as the sin of drunkenness. An analogy could be drawn between alcoholism and diabetics. A diabetic has no control over his body's inability to handle sugar. You may not be responsible for the biological predisposition to alcoholism in your body, but you are responsible for the decision not to drink, and if you have a drinking problem, to get help.

Though there is no cure for alcoholism, the disease can be arrested. However, remission is possible only through total abstinence. Combined with total abstinence, there is usually a need to restructure many aspects of a person's life both emotionally and spiritually. The alcohol-dependent person needs help and love to do that. Usually, the new beginning comes through a treatment program and then through a continuing support system where the alcohol-dependent person receives help, love and encouragement.

Alcoholics Anonymous has ten questions you can ask to determine if someone you know has a dependency problem.

1. Do you crave a drink at a definite time daily?
2. Do you gulp your drink and then sneak extras?
3. Do you drink to relieve feelings of inadequacy?
4. Do you drink to escape worry and dispel the blues?
5. Do you drink when overly tired or to "brace up"?
6. Does drinking affect your peace of mind?
7. Is drinking making your home life unhappy?
8. Do you prefer to drink alone?
9. Do you require a drink in the morning?
10. Do you lose time from work due to drinking?

If you or anyone you know can answer "yes" to even one of these questions, there is cause to be concerned and to act. It is possible to get help.

ILLEGAL DRUG DEPENDENCY

With the prevalence of illegal drugs affecting even

children as young as those in grade school, many parents are rightfully worried. As a single mom, it can be a terrifying thought that your child may be taking drugs. How would you know?

According to many drug experts, an individual who has a problem with alcohol may also have problems with illegal drugs such as marijuana, cocaine, angel dust, heroin, et cetera. Review the above signs of alcohol dependency. Most apply directly to a drug dependency also. However, some additional traits could also signal a drug dependency problem. For your child's sake, investigate carefully the causes of the following.

★ Personality change in your child. For example, a previously normal, active teen turns malicious, belligerent or reclusive.

★ Failing grades, or any significant drop in grades.

★ Delinquency, sleeping through classes, reports from teachers that your child is acting strangely or seems "strung out in class."

★ Weight loss or loss of concentration.

★ Suggestions from other parents that your child has a problem. Don't take these as insults or accusations. They could make all the difference to your child's health and well-being.

Remember that denial accompanies almost all drug dependency cases; denial by those dependent and those around them that the problem exists. Blaming your child's friends, adolescence, school, peer pressure, your divorce or the father's death won't help. It takes courage to admit, "my child is on drugs," but unless you admit it, you can't begin to get help.

If you do discover or suspect a problem, contact a parent support group. Your local mental health agencies will have recommendations for one. These tend to be excellent groups with good success rates. Especially as a single mom, you'll need their help and advice.

PRESCRIPTION DRUG DEPENDENCY

"Women learn early in life to go to a doctor and ask for a pill," said Dr. Ted Williams in a recent article in *Family Circle*. He went on to say that it is much easier for a doctor to write out a prescription than to try to deal with the cause of pain in a patient.

Statistics support his comments. Nearly 60 percent of all visits to physicians are made by women and 75 percent of all psychoactive, mood/mind altering drugs prescribed in the United States are for women. Because of this, it is estimated that one to two million women nationwide have problems related to the use of prescription drugs.

This can happen easily, especially when one is under pressure and stress. Pills seem harmless. They aren't illegal drugs or alcohol, but the results of prescription drug dependency can be equally disasterous.

In an excellent article in *Today's Christian Woman*, Katherine Lindskoog shared how she started taking Valium to ease the problems she had with multiple sclerosis. She took it at night to help her get to sleep, but the dosage kept increasing and increasing. She didn't feel like she was addicted because, "I assumed that an addiction meant a conscious craving for a certain substance. In the case of Valium that isn't true at all. I doubt that anyone ever craves Valium the way a smoker craves a cigarette." She then described the nightmare of withdrawal. Hospitalized she said, "I felt as if ants were crawling through my head." Valium withdrawal, she found out, is harder to go through than heroin withdrawal.

Valium isn't the only culprit. Pain killers, diet pills,

46

stomach calmers, cough suppressants, tranquilizers, sleeping pills—all of these bring relief for short term problems, but they can be misused. Below are questions to ask if you suspect you or someone you care about may have a problem with prescription drugs:

1. To get the same effect, do you need to take more and more of the drug?
2. Do you become overly concerned about getting the drug?
3. Do you take the drug even before symptoms occur, "just in case"?
4. Do you get prescriptions for the same drug from more than one doctor and have them filled at different places?
5. Have you ever tried to talk your doctor into refilling your prescription "just one more time"?

A "yes" to any one of these questions means you or someone you know may be dangerously drug dependent.

GETTING HELP WITH CHEMICAL DEPENDENCY PROBLEMS

There are many fine counselors and rehabilitation centers throughout the country, but an important resource for help, encouragement and spiritual counsel is your local church. Some churches have alcohol abuse counseling for family members and, if not, may know where help is available. Even if your church does not have such a program available, your pastor's counsel may give you needed support and encouragement through the difficult days of getting help for a loved one.

One of the first steps in getting help is education. Many excellent books are available and your local librarian can help you find them. Another excellent educational source are the meetings of Alcoholics Anonymous or an Al Anon group. In them, people relate their experiences. You can ask questions, share, or not say anything. They are completely confidential groups. Both organizations often have an office where you can call and ask questions, and they have a lot of excellent literature.

Al Anon is specifically designed for friends and families of people with chemical dependency problems. Many times someone with a chemical or alcohol problem has found help because a friend or family member took the time to find out enough about the problem to be able to help in a realistic way. A fairly new, but extremely beneficial offshoot of Al Anon is ACA, Adult Children of Alcoholics.

"I thought I had escaped any alcohol problems," said Lisa. "My dad was an alcoholic, but I never drank and I didn't marry an alcoholic. Then Cindy started drinking and I found out that the tendency to alcoholism can be passed on genetically through me. Because I grew up in an alcoholic home, I was an extreme perfectionist in an attempt to bring order into my life. I could not admit my daughter had a problem because this did not fit into my picture of who I was.

"Adult Children of Alcoholics has made me realize what they mean by dependency being a family disease— and acting on that realization has changed my family's life for the better."

After education comes action. Often the chemically dependent person is unable to take action on their own because of the denial that keeps them functioning. A technique that has saved many people is called "intervention." This is used in treatment centers and successful drug programs all across America.

Intervention usually begins with one or more family members contacting a professional. The family members and friends of the chemically dependent person are trained to understand that the behavior they have seen over the past months or years can be treated and changed. They are then taught to gather evidence of the person's behavior. A treatment program is found and arrangements are made to admit the person. A meeting is then set where the family members and the professional gently, but firmly, confront the chemically dependent person with his actions while under the influence of the drug or alcohol. The person is then told that arrangements have been made for him to enter a treatment program.

These interventions are difficult, but the results can be powerful.

One man, who now heads an alcoholic recovery group, talked about his intervention. "When my eight-year-old son told me I was a drunk, I couldn't believe it. I thought my drinking was social and okay," he said.

"My mom is eighty," said Ann, as she told me about the growing problems of alcohol abuse among the elderly. "I scheduled the intervention. It was the hardest thing I've ever done. Mom's pastor came along. When confronted, she agreed she had a problem, but when we told her we were taking her for treatment, she said she'd rather go in a few weeks. Pastor James told her, 'No, Mary, the arrangements are all made, you're going now.' It helped to have him there."

Betty Ford, whose treatment center for chemical dependency has enabled many of the rich and famous to face their addiction problems, credits the start of her recovery to an intervention staged by her family. They confronted her with her problems with chemical abuse.

After intervention comes a treatment program. If the addiction is severe, this usually involves hospitalization. The hospitalization will begin with a detoxification program designed to cleanse the person's body of the harmful chemicals. Next comes a reeducation program in which the person is taught how to live a drug-free life. The entire family is involved in this part of the program. Finally, some sort of aftercare is begun in a group that will encourage the addicted person to stay away from the substance that first caused the problem.

HOPE

While working on this book, I attended several Alcoholics Anonymous and Al Anon meetings. I expected to see sad, struggling people. While the people there, along with their families, were working hard to change their lives, they were anything but sad. Again and again I saw hope. I saw joy. I heard people actually thank God for the problem of drug dependency in their lives. Why? Because once they faced it, it forced them to depend on God in a way they never had before and to change many areas of their lives.

If there is any sort of a chemical dependency problem in your life or in the life of your children, face it. Learn about it, and get help. Our God is a God of new beginnings. Give Him a chance to begin again with you.

RESOURCES

The following booklets are basic ones which explain chemical dependency. Each is excellent. They are published by one of the leading authorities on the problem of chemical dependency, the Johnson Institute. For prices and a listing of numerous other publications they offer, write or call:

JOHNSON INSTITUTE
10700 Olson Memorial Highway
Minneapolis, MN 55441-6199
612-544-4156

RECOMMENDED BOOKLETS:

Chemical Dependency and Recovery Are a Family Affair

Alcoholism, a Treatable Disease

Intervention

If one of your parents had a problem with alcohol or drugs, I highly recommend *It Could Never Happen to Me* by Claudia Black.

Local groups of Al Anon, Alcoholics Anonymous, and associated groups that deal with drug dependency such as Narcotics Anonymous can all be found in the phone directory. You can check in the Yellow Pages of your phone directory for a listing of Alcoholism Information & Treatment Centers. Or in the White Pages under Alcohol for an Alcoholics Anonymous listing. If there is no local AA write to: P.O. Box 459, Grand Central Station, New York, New York 10163. Ask for the list of AA central and intergroup offices in the U.S. and Canada.

"Precious in the sight of the Lord is the death of his saints."
Psalm 116:15, KJV

5

DEATH

"The last enemy to be destroyed is death .... When the perishable has been clothed with the imperishable, and the mortal with immortality, then the saying that is written will come true: 'Death has been swallowed up in victory.'

" 'Where, O death, is your victory? Where, O death, is your sting?' The sting of death is sin, and the power of sin is the law. But thanks be to God! He gives us the victory through our Lord Jesus Christ."
I Corinthians 15:26,54-57

One of the saddest things about human death is that it is so terribly lonely. For a single woman, facing death alone may seem almost too much to bear. When I thought about this I remembered the comfort Psalm 23:1 always gave me as a child when I was afraid to go to sleep by myself at night: "The Lord is my shepherd."

As an adult, realizing that I might have to face some of the hardest times of life and maybe even my own death without someone I loved beside me, the rest of that psalm took on a new meaning for me. It goes on to say, *"Yea, though I walk through the valley of the shadow of death, I will fear no evil: for thou art with me"* (Psalm 23:4, KJV). The Bible never says that we won't experience horribly painful moments in life, but God does tell us that we never are alone. Even when we let go of life, our Lord never lets go of our hand.

FACING THE END OF A MARRIAGE

Are you having a hard time forgetting?

Do you feel guilty because you still cry over the love you lost—either by death or divorce? No matter how or when it happens, it isn't easy to get over a love that once filled your life.

I used to envy widows. I felt like they, at least, had the approval of society and the church to grieve. I struggled with so much guilt and shame over the breakup of my marriage by divorce, that I didn't know what to do about the sadness. I felt that I had no right to cry. Yet, there were times when I would cry and cry for the simple loss of a relationship that had defined my life for thirteen years. Then one day a wise friend shared with me that, though the person I was married to still lived, the relationship had died. And therein was my permission to cry.

By death or divorce, a marriage dies and that is cause to grieve. Grief is painful and lengthy. A loss in one area can trigger memories of losses in other areas of life and the cumulative effect can be devastating. If we don't get over our loss quickly, we feel society and the church will become impatient.

But sometimes recovery doesn't come in the allotted 18 months or so. As Martha Yates puts it in her book,

Coping: "There would be months—no, years—ahead of self-delusion, when I would tell myself that he wasn't really dead, and that he would come back to me. I have run the length of a shopping mall because I thought I saw him at the other end. I have followed a car for miles until I could see the driver again, because he had turned his head as George had. I have answered the telephone expecting to hear his beloved voice on the other end of the wire."

Her experiences are not unique.

A recent study by the University of Michigan suggests that traditional notions about grief need to be re-examined and that, for many, the grieving process may take far longer than we have previously expected. The study found that four to seven years after the death of a spouse or a child, most survivors still hadn't put the loss behind them. The study also concluded that they "shouldn't be blamed for not recovering from their grief more quickly."

A radio talk show recently told a call-in guest that, "old loves never die, they just live in a quieter place." That thought comforted me when happy memories of a life that was gone were troubling.

If you have been feeling guilty because you still grieve over the death of your marriage, don't dwell on your guilt and don't be angry or impatient with yourself. No wound heals if you constantly trouble it. Grief is an emotion that goes away silently as you concentrate on other things. Fill your life with other things, and though you will never forget a love that has died, it will someday live in a quieter place.

PREPARING FOR YOUR OWN DEATH

Much of what is written on estate planning and the importance of having a will is directed to married couples, but it is just as important for a single woman. If you have minor children, it is critical. But even if you don't, without proper estate planning, you could cost friends and family much time, pain and expense.

The cost of dying is at an all time high and will probably go higher. The average cost of a traditional funeral today is over $3,000.00. Other expenses include cemetery space, mausoleum, marker, any medical expenses or legal fees. You cannot just quietly die in America. No matter how much or little you have, the courts will be involved. The government will notice. The laws that govern death are not just for people with a lot of money.

In addition to the courts, your death will involve many others. Be sure to have the following information in a place easily accessible to your spouse substitute.

★ names and addresses of those to be notified

★ insurance benefits and insurance papers

★ eligibility for federal benefits.

★ any other facts or papers affecting your specific situation. See chapter on Organization.

WHAT HAPPENS IF YOU DIE WITHOUT A WILL?

Your checking and other accounts are frozen and your bank box sealed. Someone, usually your family, will have to pay for all the legal expenses involved in settling your estate. It is not an option to use the courts for this. It's mandatory.

Without a will the courts would decide who gets your inheritance, however small or large, after lengthy appraisals of it. The line of inheritance may vary from state to state, but it often goes first to brothers and sisters, then to parents. Often, parents on fixed income can be left out and the money given to siblings at the peak of their earning years. Or, after court fees, there could be nothing at all for family, friends or favorite charities.

If you have children and die without a will (intestate), the court will appoint a guardian. This guardian will be responsible to the court for every action taken for them. And it may not be the person you would have wanted. This person would also have to post an expensive bond and much time could be spent in court reporting actions taken with regard to the children.

Your family would be responsible for all funeral and burial expenses until the courts decided how to disburse your money. Your personal effects would probably have to be appraised and sold, and they may not be given to family members.

There are many horror stories of family struggles when a person has died without a will. Catherine Marshall in her book, *To Live Again*, tells of the trauma she went through when her famous husband died without a will. She tells of how it took the lawyers over four months just to figure out the value of his sermons. Though they weren't worth much in monetary value, it cost a lot to have this appraisal done. She tells of how she had to report to the court every action taken for her son. She relates how legal fees ate up every penny they had. This would not have happened if her husband had left a will. But, like so many people, he didn't think that he had enough to make it worthwhile. He did not realize the cost to everyone to settle an estate, no matter how big or how small. Catherine Marshall states that after what she went through, she immediately made her own will and urged all of her friends to do the same.

Though the consequences are serious, seven out of ten people still die without a will and cause untold heartache for their families and friends by doing it.

"Me get a will?" Joyce laughed when we talked about

it. "I hardly make enough to pay the rent."

What she and many others do not realize is that a will is especially critical if the estate is not large. Probate could cost far more than the worth of your estate if it has to be settled by the courts. Family and friends may end up paying fees that would not be necessary if you had left a simple will.

This section will not tell you how to prepare a will because the specifics vary from state to state. You should see a lawyer to make sure that you do things properly. But, hopefully, this section will give you some things to consider.

First of all, a single person should select someone to act in place of a spouse in the financial and legal dealings involving a will and final wishes. For instance, my mother is a widow and, as I am a single woman, we acted in this capacity for one another. You should share with this person the overall details of your financial life, or at least where a listing of your debts and assets could be found upon your death. That person should also have a key to your safety deposit box. Since checking accounts are sealed upon death, it is not a bad idea to have a small life insurance policy made out to this person to take care of final expenses. Life insurance policies pay immediately upon death. They are not frozen like many other assets are, and they are one of the best ways to take care of final costs.

You should then select a lawyer and, with your spouse substitute, go to him to make your will. It is a good idea to have your wishes written out before you go. This gives you time to organize your thoughts and make changes at far less cost than if you do all your thinking in the lawyer's office. If you decide to have your friend be the administrator of your will, first make sure he or she understands the responsibilities involved. The lawyer can explain these in detail. Then, be sure you state in your will that no bond is required.

If you have children or a large estate, you may want to establish a trust. A trust will guarantee that your money will be spent in the way you wish after you are gone. The basic principle of a trust is simple: You turn over a certain amount of money or property to an individual or institution to be kept, used and administered by the trustees for the benefit of the beneficiary. For example, you can set up a trust with a bank by giving them an amount of money and specify that your children will get a set income until they are a certain age. The principle may be simple, but it can become quite complex, so get good legal advice. The trust department of your local bank can advise you concerning this. Check with friends or family members for a reference to a good estate lawyer. Or, check with your local Bar Association for a referral.

WHAT IF YOU SHOULD BECOME INCAPACITATED

"But what happens if you don't die?"

I was sitting in a seminar on financial planning for women. After discussing why we, as women, needed our own wills, the leader caught all of our attention with this question.

In an effort not to think about difficult decisions, we tend to push unpleasant thoughts out of our minds. Sometimes we escape by thinking things like, "Oh well, I'll just die. Then nobody will worry about me anymore, and I won't be around to care what happens."

The truth is that few people die suddenly. Most often, at some point prior to death, there is a time when many of us will not be able to care for ourselves or our finances. With this in mind, my mother wisely set up, with her lawyer, what in our state is a type of power of attorney. This will allow me, along with her lawyer, to pay her bills and make financial decisions if she is unable to do so.

The guidelines are set up now. The paperwork is all in place. We have discussed it carefully.

No matter what your age, you should make similar plans because an automobile or other accident could happen at any time. While doing that, it is a good idea to think through two additional areas.

The first is organ donation. Many people have regained their sight and hearing as beneficiaries of this program. Many others are able to live normal lives free from expensive kidney machines because someone marked a small space on their driver's license that allowed organ parts to be donated to someone who needed them in the event of death. A call to the Department of Motor Vehicles or your local eye bank will give you more information on the proper procedure for organ donation.

The second area concerns your wishes regarding life support systems and the heroic or extraordinary measures which may be used to keep a patient alive. Many states have what is called a "Living Will." By this, individuals who do not wish to be put on life support systems sign a document which indicates this and have it notarized. The legal status of these documents varies greatly, but once you make a decision, it is a good idea to communicate your wishes to your family doctor and lawyer. You may even want to leave a copy of the document on file with both of these individuals.

FUNERAL PLANNING

It is critical to be prepared for one's death from a spiritual viewpoint, but from a human standpoint, preparation for death should also include the financial aspects. By carefully preplanning your own funeral arrangements and those of the ones for whom you are responsible, you can save between 50-75 percent in costs and inestimable amounts of heartache for your family.

One of the best helps in funeral planning is to join a memorial society. This is not a prepaid funeral plan. Memorial societies are consumer groups that obtain funeral arrangements which reflect simplicity, dignity and economy. There are approximately 750,000 memorial society members throughout the United States.

"After I joined the memorial society, I felt so at ease," Jenny shared. "I paid a small, one-time fee and then they sent me forms to fill out which listed my funeral plans, relatives, et cetera. They have an arrangement with a local funeral home and the prices are set for members. You decide ahead of time what you want and that way your family knows. You carry a little card with you so someone can notify them at the time of death. It's really simple and it sure solves a lot of potential problems."

I found my own experience with a memorial society to be equally pleasant. They have reciprocal arrangements with societies all over the United States, Canada and in some foreign countries. To find out about the one nearest you, write to: Continental Association of Funeral and Memorial Societies, 1828 L Street N. W., Washington, DC 20036.

As a single woman, you may find yourself alone and responsible for the funeral plans of parents or other family members. In addition to joining a memorial society, one of the best resources for death education is a little book entitled, *A Manual of Death Education and Simple Burial*, by Ernest Morgan. It can be ordered from Celo Press, Burnsville, North Carolina 28714. It is one of the most helpful books I have ever read and I cannot recommend it enough. It contains valuable information on death education, funeral planning, memorial societies, organ donation and related topics.

Additional Recommended Reading:

A Manual of Death Education and Simple Burial
  by Ernest Morgan
By Death or Divorce... It Hurts to Lose
  by Amy Ross Mumford

"Whatever you do, work at it with all your heart, as working for the Lord, not for men."

Colossians 3:23, NIV

6

EMPLOYMENT

Employment for women today is in one of those "good news, bad news" situations.

The good news is that never before have so many jobs been open to women. Far from the days when certain occupations were not considered ladylike, a woman today is encouraged to undertake any career.

Statistics like these are the bad news:

—Women still make only $.60 to every $1.00 men make.

—In the same job, women earn 25-40 percent less than a man.

—One out of every four separated or divorced women is on welfare.

—One out of every three families headed by a woman is living below the poverty line.

Whether the job market is good news or bad news to you, as a single woman you will most likely need to work. This chapter will give you ideas in a number of job related areas. First, it'll help you set some overall goals for your work life. Then you'll get some specific advice on how to decide what your skills are. Finally, you'll find hints on how to write a resume and conduct yourself at a job interview.

In addition to the information in this chapter, check at your local women's center or community college. Many of them have re-entry programs for women starting back into the work force. I took one at my local community college and it was excellent. In addition to giving me lots of good advice, meeting other women in a similar situation was very encouraging.

FIRST THINGS FIRST

"I panicked," said Joyce, when she described her realization that she had to support herself and her son after her husband left her. "I ran from one employment agency to another. I'd take a temporary job; then I'd quit. I needed to make more money, but I didn't know what to do."

It took Joyce several years, lots of trial, error and frustration to become happy in her work and to make an adequate living for herself and her son. She finally found a field she loved—nutrition. She had to go back to school for additional training, which was difficult, but now she is doing something, "that I can be happy in and grow in for the rest of my life," she says.

Her case is typical for many newly single women. Younger women today are raised thinking about careers, but many women who become single in their late thirties through fifties grew up thinking about husbands and babies rather than making career plans. To be single again takes a whole new readjustment to life. There is often confusion and the tendency to take any job, just to pay the bills, until a man can come along to take care of you again. Many never married women feel the same. A job is just a temporary situation until they find Prince Charming.

In addition to this being an unhealthy psychological attitude toward life, to think like that negates how precious your life and career are to God. Male and female, we are all parts of His kingdom and He has work for us to do with the skills and talents He has entrusted to us. A lot of job dissatisfaction for both men and women comes from forgetting to ask God, "what did you create me for? Where in your world can I do the job you have planned for me?"

As you seek to find God's will in your career choice, don't limit yourself to specifically Christian jobs. Though God does call many people into church related jobs, look at some of the job descriptions in the Bible. Abraham was a wealthy shepherd. David ruled a kingdom. Ruth was a part-time farm laborer. Deborah was a ruler and judge. Lydia was a successful businesswoman. The list could go on and on. The idea of full-time Christian work is a fairly recent one in the history of God's people. Sometimes I wonder if God didn't have to start calling people into that sort of job because they were forgetting that in whatever they do, they were to do it to God's glory and to be His witnesses.

Finally, don't let the press of financial need settle you into a career choice that isn't right for you. You may need to work on two levels as you seek more schooling. You may have to take a job just to keep bread on the table while you pray, plan and train for your ultimate career and calling.

HOW TO FIND THE JOB FOR YOU

If you haven't worked for awhile, or are unhappy in your present job, you may have never really thought about what you want to do. Below are several suggestions to help you decide. Some will apply to your situation, some won't. In whatever you do, ask for God's guidance. Ask that He work in your thought processes, in the events that happen outside your control. Throughout the entire process, keep these promises in mind:

> *And thine ears shall hear a word behind thee, saying, This is the way, walk ye in it, when ye turn to the right hand, and when ye turn to the left.*
> Isaiah 30:21, KJV

> *I will instruct thee and teach thee in the way which thou shalt go: I will guide thee with mine eye.*
> Psalm 32:8, KJV

> *The meek will he guide in judgment: and the meek will he teach his way.*
> Psalm 25:9, KJV

Remembering that your career is tremendously important to God, try these ideas:

★ See if your local community college or women's center offers career testing. Romans 12 says that we should have an honest evaluation of ourselves. This is an important first step in making any career decision. These tests are fun to take and you often find out things you didn't know about yourself. Along with taking the tests, you usually get to talk to a job counselor about the results and that can give you additional insight.

★ Write down every job, even little ones, volunteer or paid, that you have had. Write down what you liked about them, what you didn't. Look for patterns. Do you prefer to work with people or things? Do you like to be in charge or do you like someone else to do the worrying? Are you good at detail work or are you better with the big picture? Then think about the kind of jobs that fit these characteristics. For example, if you work best quietly and alone, you probably wouldn't make a good receptionist.

★ Think through what characteristics are important to you in a job. Some areas to consider are: job stability, income, status, creativity, responsibility. If stability is very important to you, don't take a commission only job. If you love to be creative, assembly line work is not for you.

★ Look at your hobbies and volunteer activities. Numerous women have turned craft ideas into money making ventures. Volunteer activities can easily turn into full-time jobs. One woman I know did lots of volunteer work for veterans' wives and widows, helping them find out their benefits. When the local veterans' office had an opening for a counselor, she was offered the job.

★ As you consider certain jobs, be realistic about the training needed. There are all sorts of part-time training programs, week-end programs and refresher courses. Check on them. A number of the women I met in the re-entry course I took, finished college and went to graduate school after becoming widows. It is never too late to do what you have always wanted to do. Also find out about financial aid programs. Although they are harder to get than they used to be, you never know until you check.

★ Also, be realistic about the physical limitations of a job. I think this is often forgotten and shouldn't be because God is in control here also. I know one woman who makes a good living cleaning houses. She is very strong physically. I have another friend who is a massage therapist. Again, she is quite strong. Another friend has to travel extensively with her job. She arrives half-way across the country fresh and ready to work. These women all amaze me. I have had surgeries and major illnesses all my life. If I were stronger, I'd probably be out doing something I consider far more exciting than what I am doing, but I know God wants me to be a writer. I can write in the hospital, or just after surgery or when I have pneumonia. And I have in all these situations. Not many other jobs would put up with me.

★ Some community college career counseling centers send students out to interview people in jobs they think they will like. This accomplishes several purposes. First of all, you get to see what a job is like from someone actually doing it in your town and you can ask in-depth questions about it. Second, people get to know you. If you are very interested, you can always ask if they would let you know if there is a job opening.

★ A variation of the suggestion above is to work for temporary job services for awhile. This not only provides an income, but gives you a chance to try different kinds of work and to become known in various businesses. Many permanent jobs have come from temporary assignments.

★ Finally, be realistic about what a job pays. Some jobs will never pay enough for you to make a decent living even though they require quite a bit of work and training. Find out the future of a job before you prepare for it. If it is something you really enjoy, perhaps a slightly different kind of work will enable you to make a living wage. For example, if you want to teach and work with children, you may want to work toward a teaching certificate rather than a teacher's aid job.

JOB IDEAS

The variety of jobs available today is astounding. To

find some of them, don't just look through the want ads. Look through the yellow pages of your phone book, too. You'll be amazed at what people do to make a living. Eighty percent of all jobs available are not listed either in the want ads or by employment agencies. Here are some places to contact or think about:

★ The federal government is the nation's single largest employer. They also tend to offer some of the greatest job security. Your state employment office will have civil service and other government job listings. They will also be able to tell you how to apply for these jobs and what tests you might have to take.

★ There are numerous nonprofit organizations for whom you might want to work. In addition to numerous Christian organizations, there are all sorts of groups that work with consumer affairs, troubled children, the handicapped, et cetera. If you are interested, go visit them. These places rarely advertise for people. Find out the kinds of skills you could offer them. You may need to do some volunteer work there for a time in order for them to get to know you.

★ InterCristo is an international Christian organization that places Christians in jobs all over the world. If interested, write to them at 19303 Fremont Avenue N., Seattle, Washington, 98133.

★ Think up your own job. One very exciting thing that has happened in the job market for women is a booming business in completely new areas. Women are very creative. This is most apparent in some of the new service industries some women have created. House-cleaning services are now big business. Some services purchase groceries and plan meals and parties. There are other purchasing services from gift buying to wardrobe shopping. Some women run chauffeuring services, others run errands and pick up kids. The service industry potential is only as limited as your imagination.

If you want to start your own business, the Small Business Administration of the federal government has a booklet entitled, *Women's Handbook*. To obtain a copy write to: Office of Women's Business Ownership, 1441 L Street, NW, Washington, DC 20416.

HOW TO WRITE A RESUME

This is a sort of extended calling card. It tells who you are, what job you want, and why you qualify for it. And, it isn't hard to write if you follow the tips below:

★ You can't write one all-purpose resume. Tailor your resume for the job you are seeking. By tailoring the resume for the job, you can emphasize the skills and experiences which qualify you for the particular position. Remember that the best resumes are only a page or two long. To tailor a resume for a job, concentrate on the experiences that are pertinent for that job and leave others out. For example, when I applied for part-time teaching jobs, I listed my previous teaching jobs. I didn't go into detail about the little candlemaking company I started in college or my experiences as a waitress.

★ A resume is a great means of self-evaluation. It will help organize your thoughts concerning your experiences, accomplishments, and related education before a job interview.

★ Always be 100 percent honest in a resume. Be correct about dates, the addresses and phone numbers of references, salaries, et cetera.

★ After you have drafted your resume, attempt to be objective and ask yourself, what does this tell me about

70

the person who wrote it? Would I want to hire this person?

★ The reference desk at your local library can guide you to books that have many examples of written resumes. These are very helpful. They will show you how, for example, to take home or volunteer work and list it in a professional way.

If you don't have access to a source such as this, the basic resume should include the following topics:

1. Name, address and phone number
2. Objective—the type of job you want
3. Summary of qualifications—include education, work experience and personal qualifications. Again, do not make this exhaustive. Just list things which apply to the particular job.
4. Awards and memberships if pertinent
5. References—include addresses and phone numbers

You don't have to have your resume professionally printed. A neat typing job is fine.

WHAT TO DO AT A JOB INTERVIEW

One of the best ways to prepare for an interview is to find out all you can about the company in question. See if they have any background histories or brochures available from their Public Relations department or the local library. If you know people who work there, talk to them. Know why you want the job and why you want to work for that particular company. Then practice with a friend.

The personnel manager for a major company in Colorado gives the following tips for a successful interview:

1. Be aware that many companies will conduct a brief phone interview first. Be prepared for it. Have notes by your phone. Ask a friend to call and ask you questions based on your resume. Then have that person give you feedback on how you sound.

2. Find out who you will be interviewing with and their responsibilities so you can react with them in a knowledgeable way.

3. Interviewers look for self-confidence, maturity, a sense of humor, ability to express yourself, warmth, and an ability to communicate.

4. Do not dress improperly, ask about salary, act threatened or like you want to take over.

5. Act confident and react to the interviewer's questions simply as another person. They probably wouldn't even interview you if they didn't think you already had the basic qualifications.

FINAL ENCOURAGEMENTS

It is easy to get discouraged when looking for work. You have to think of getting a job as a full-time job in itself. But when that job consists of rejection after rejection, it can be difficult.

Don't give up. You have to work. Think of interviewing as a challenge. Think of it as learning to press on even when you don't feel like it. Think of it as a time to trust God and to exercise your faith. Keep in mind Jeremiah 29:11:

> *"For I know the plans I have for you,"*
> *declares the Lord, "plans to prosper you*
> *and not to harm you, plans to give you*
> *hope and a future."*

72

Additional Recommended Reading:

What to Do With the Rest of Your Life
   by the Catalyst Staff
The Professional Resume and Job Search Guide
   by Harold W. Dickhut
Entrepreneurial Mothers by Phyllis Gillis

"A merry heart doeth good like a medicine: but a broken spirit drieth the bones."

Proverbs 17:22, KJV

7

HEALTH

"The preservation of health is a duty. Few seem conscious that there is such a thing as physical morality."
Herbert Spencer, Education

I like that comment. So often our health is something that we don't think about. We go about our daily lives, eating whatever we want, not exercising, overworking and worrying. Then we get sick and wonder what went wrong. It is especially easy for single women to become careless about their health. By nature we tend to be caretakers of others, but we often don't take very good care of ourselves.

I like Spencer's emphasis on the duty to preserve health. Though we acknowledge the ultimate control of God over every aspect of our lives, there is a lot we can do to make the best use of the bodies He has given us. In the same way that we are responsible to use our material resources and gifts in the best way possible, even so we have a responsibility to use our bodies in the best way possible. That is the essence of this chapter.

THREE KINDS OF HEALTH

I like things in nice, tidy compartments. My drawers, closets and cabinets all follow the rule of "a place for everything and everything in its place." But one part of life I've learned not to divide into separate compartments is my health.

I want to do that. If I hurt or am ill, I want to take a pill and make it all better. Period. I don't want to look at my lifestyle, my spiritual life or my attitudes and resentments. Yet, our bodies don't work that way. God made each of us a whole person with three parts: body, soul and mind. We can't just ignore one part if we truly want to experience total health. With this realization in mind, this chapter is divided into physical, spiritual and psychological health with suggestions on how to be good stewards of each part.

PHYSICAL HEALTH

Just as our total health is divided into several areas, our physical health can be divided into how we take care of our diet and how we exercise.

DIET

"Jeff told me he ate sauerkraut and eggs for dinner. I told him I had sardines and an apple." June laughed as she told me this. "I don't imagine anybody eats worse than single people."

I had to agree. I, of all people, ought to eat better I kept telling myself. I write books about nutrition. But without someone else for whom to cook, I found myself grazing through the kitchen, eating whatever I could find whenever I felt like it. My health started to suffer because of it, and my weight began to fluctuate erratically. I finally got strict with myself and below are some of the guidelines I found useful in helping me to eat healthfully as a single person.

1) Learn what constitutes a healthful diet. Read or reread some books on nutrition; take a natural foods cooking class; read some magazine articles on healthful cooking.

In brief, some of the most important aspects of a healthful diet are:

- Avoid foods you know aren't good for you—candy, sugared items, too much fat, too much caffeine or salt.
- Try to eat a diet high in fiber, or what we used to call roughage. This means whole grain cereals, salads, apples and almonds, anything with whole wheat.
- Be sure to eat foods high in calcium. Most women don't get enough and their bones become soft. This causes many problems as they get older. An excellent source of calcium is milk products. If you eat yogurt as a source of calcium, you also get the beneficial aspects of the yogurt bacteria which include better digestion, better iron absorption, and protection against a number of other health problems.

- Try to eat a variety of foods. As a single, it's easy to live on a few favorite items—especially if you don't have children for whom to cook. But peanut butter and celery, plus coffee and diet pop do not make a balanced diet.
- Take a multiple vitamin as added protection. I fully agree with the nutritional experts that if you eat a well-balanced diet of healthful foods, you can get all the nutrients you need. But, realistically, who does that? Especially since women frequently diet, chances are you aren't eating the volume of foods you need to supply all your nutritional needs.
- If you need help, encouragement or just tasty recipes, my cookbooks, *Guilt-Free Cooking, Guilt-Free Snacking* and *Guilt-Free Fast Foods*, contain healthy, easy-to-cook foods for single people. All are published by Accent Books, Denver, Colorado.

2) Once you know the basics of good nutrition, buy only healthful foods. Then, don't worry too much about how you fix them or when you eat if you are on an erratic schedule. For example, if you have fish, vegetables, fruit, whole grain bread, nuts and dried fruit, milk and yogurt around the house, no matter what you fix, it is bound to be good for you. If you don't buy junk, you won't be tempted to eat junk.

3) Consider a microwave. They are great for single people. They are a big investment, but if you use one regularly, it will save a lot on eating out costs. My mother, who is a widow, wouldn't do without hers. She can fix a large casserole or similar food and freeze meal-size portions in small containers. When she wants a main dish entree in a hurry, she just has to thaw and heat one of them.

4) Buy popcorn. As a single person I could not live without popcorn. To me it is a perfect food. It's very cheap

(don't buy the fancy brands), and easy to prepare. At only 50 calories per cup, it is a great carbohydrate-comfort food but without the guilt of chocolate. You can have it for a snack any time of the day or night, and it tastes even better when it's a day old. You can serve it to guests when you have nothing else. Dogs like it and so do birds. It's completely natural, has no additives, contains fiber and doesn't cause cancer. What more could you ask for?

EXERCISE

A recent Food and Drug Administration publication stated that most overweight problems result from, "a relatively tiny imbalance between daily energy intake and expenditure." Only 50 to 100 extra calories a day— one extra tablespoon of butter—can add several pounds a year. At the same time, one-half hour of moderate exercise not only burns off those additional calories, but gives the benefit of increased overall health also.

The saying, "no pain, no gain," might be true for Olympic athletes in training, but it is not true for the average person. Exercise is for everyone at every age, but you must adjust the types of exercise you do to your age and health. I have had two knee surgeries. I can no longer run, so I ride an exercise bicycle and swim. Walking is an excellent exercise for anyone. If regular aerobics are difficult for you, try swimnastics—aerobic exercises done standing in water. The water takes the weight off your joints, and makes it much less harmful.

Once you have decided you want to exercise, you next have to decide if you want to exercise by yourself at home, or if you want to join some sort of spa, health or exercise club.

EXERCISING AT HOME

If you exercise at home, you don't have to take the extra time to go somewhere else. It costs less, and you never have to worry about your health facility being closed. You can also make maximum use of your exercise time. For example, I read the newspaper and magazines each day while on my exercise bike. I like it because I can catch up on my reading and exercise at the same time.

There is a lot of good home exercise equipment available today from exercise bicycles and rowing machines to all sorts of sophisticated equipment. Go to a reputable store, ask for recommendations, and try them out before making a purchase. If possible, get a visitor's pass to a health club and try out all the equipment while there.

Some disadvantages to exercising at home are that you will probably not work out as consistently or as hard as you would if you were committed to working out a certain number of times a week at some sort of class or club. You also may not use equipment properly, and you probably won't have things like saunas and whirlpools at home. They are a nice reward after working out.

EXERCISING AT A HEALTH CLUB

If you decide you want to work out at a health club, there are a number of factors to consider before joining one. They include:

1. First of all, decide why you want to join a health club. Being a single woman, it is important to decide if you want to use the facility as a place to meet men, if you even want to be around them, or if you just want to work

out. Some women like the easy companionship of health clubs as a place to meet men on a purely friendship level. "It's great," Joanne told me. "I've met some very nice men, and several of them have become good friends."

That's wonderful for her, but I look lumpy in my leotard which is eight years old and not one of the new, designer color-coordinated ones. My hair is usually dirty, and I wear no make-up when I go work out. To me, exercise is enough torture without having to worry if my mascara is running or not. For these reasons, I prefer women only clubs.

2. Once that decision is made, decide what facilities you want, and shop around for a club. I have to have a swimming pool. Some people need an indoor track. I love a sauna and whirlpool. Some people like to just attend an exercise class, shower and leave. There is a wide variety around today. Find one that suits your needs.

3. Find one that is close enough to your work or your home so distance won't be an excuse for not using it.

4. Be sure you get a few guest passes and visit before you join. Notice how crowded it is, how clean it is and how knowledgeable the staff is. Never, under any circumstances, feel pressured to join because of some great deal the first time you visit. If it is a reputable firm, the price will be fairly consistent. Take the contract home, comparison shop, and think about it before you make your decision.

BEWARE OF THESE THINGS

You've seen the advertisements:
"The perfect pill—lose weight without dieting!"
"Try a body wrap and lose inches within the hour!"

"New latex exercising suit, double your weight loss during exercise!"

We're all tempted by the promise of instant health and beauty. Who wouldn't buy something if it really would take off those unwanted pounds without all the work of diet and exercise. But, as a recent FDA bulletin pointed out, "The pill or shot that enables a person to lose weight without danger or without eating less has not been formulated. And the garment or other device to let one firm up or lose inches without moving a muscle has yet to be invented."

The body wraps and exercise suits show a loss of inches because of perspiration. And the pills, particularly of such exotic types as the recent "starch blockers," not only do not actually help weight loss, but can cause nausea, vomiting, diarrhea and stomach pains.

When you are alone it is easy to be vulnerable to this sort of thing. Just remember there are no short cuts to health or weight loss. Doing the proper things, day by day, step by step, is the way to success.

WHEN HEALTH FAILS

No matter what you do, there are bound to be times when you become sick. This can be very scary if you are living by yourself. It is important to tell a friend when you aren't feeling well, even if it is something that doesn't seem to be serious.

"I thought I just had a little case of the flu," said Janey, "but then I started throwing up and got so dehydrated and weak that I couldn't even get to the phone. If Amy hadn't come by to check on me and take me to the hospital, I don't know what would have happened."

When I heard her story, I realized the same thing could

have happened to me with my little habit of not wanting to bother anyone when I don't feel well. Put your pride and self-sufficiency aside and prepare for illness ahead of time. Agree with a friend that you will play nursemaid when she is sick and have her do the same for you. This could include:

★ Calling to check in once or twice a day at pre-determined times. If you don't come to the phone, she would know to come over or have a neighbor check to see what is wrong.

★ Buying groceries for you and making sure you eat, even if you don't feel like it.

★ Taking you to the doctor—you shouldn't drive yourself if you are ill or taking certain medications.

★ One of the most wonderful things you can do for a person who has been sick is to clean house for her. It's hard to be ill and watch your house and laundry grow into a bigger and bigger mess. Once, after a painful wrist surgery, when I got out of the hospital a friend arrived at my door, told me to lay down and she cleaned my house for me. I have never forgotten that kindness.

★ Pray for and encourage one another. Illness is frightening. Our body seems to betray us and we can't do so many things that seem essential. It is frustrating when we try to do all the right things and, because we are human, we get sick. At the same time, our health isn't out of the control of God. Job's illness taught him lessons about God, and I've found that in the times I've been ill, God has always had something to teach me. Pray with your friend for patience and wisdom to discover and learn that lesson.

SPIRITUAL HEALTH

> *Therefore, I urge you, brothers, in view of God's mercy, to offer your bodies as living sacrifices, holy and pleasing to God—which is your spiritual worship. Do not conform any longer to the pattern of this world, but be transformed by the renewing of your mind. Then you will be able to test and approve what God's will is—his good, pleasing and perfect will.*
> Romans 12:1,2

The world has a plan for single women—it revolves around getting. Getting beautiful, getting successful, getting sex, getting a man. God also has a plan for single women and it involves giving. Giving yourself first to God and His plans, and then giving yourself in service to a hurting world.

God's plan and standards for your life do not change when you are single. You can't eat junk food and not expect it to harm your physical health. In the same way, there are necessary elements in spiritual health that are as necessary as the needed elements for physical health. We've all heard of the basic four food groups that we need to eat. Below are four basic spiritual groups for a healthy relationship with God.

GROUP NUMBER ONE—THE BIBLE

God's viewpoint, His way of doing things, His love and His guidance are different from anything we hear on TV or get from advertising or secular reading. In the Bible we find out God's way of life and standards.

But God's Word isn't like a first aid kit—good only for emergencies and depression. It's more like meat and potatoes—essential for living a life pleasing to God. Only by reading it daily can its teachings permeate your life. Then, when difficult times come, you will know how to respond. Find a plan that will help you structure your day to include a time with God. One guide I found helpful is *The Daily Walk*. You read a passage from the Bible and then there are comments on it. It is available from: The Navigator's Daily Walk, P.O. Box 6000, Colorado Springs, Colorado 80934. There are many other devotionals and study guides out. Check your local Christian bookstore. Find the one that fits you best.

GROUP NUMBER TWO—PRAYER

God speaks to His children through the Bible and we talk to Him through prayer. As a single person, one of the hardest things is not having someone with whom we can talk, but in prayer we can pour out our hearts to God. He is always there. Read through the Psalms. David felt free to pray about anything and everything and so should you.

You might try reading some books on prayer. Keep a prayer diary where you write down your prayer requests and God's answers. Or, pray with a friend once a week. We wouldn't think of trying to develop a relationship with another person without ever talking to them, and we can't develop a relationship with God without talking to Him. We all know that good communication is the key to a good relationship, and the more intimate, honest and total our communication to God is, the better our relationship with Him will be.

GROUP NUMBER THREE—FELLOWSHIP

For better or worse, God put us on earth to fellowship in a body, His church. Though there are times when I must confess to God that I'm glad He likes some of His other kids because I'm having a hard time with them, we have to learn to live together.

Going to church is essential for good fellowship. If you don't feel welcome at your church as a single, speak to the pastor and some close friends about it. Some non-single people just don't know what to do with a single person. Contact other singles and start a singles group if there is not one in your church. If that doesn't seem to work, prayerfully consider looking for a new church. There are many churches today that encourage and welcome single people.

GROUP NUMBER FOUR—SERVING

Many churches are sensitive to the needs of single people and already have singles classes. In them single people can meet and share, be encouraged and grow. Caring churches also minister to single people. But there is an important benefit of singleness that should not be neglected. Single people, above all others, are those most able to serve God because of their lack of obligations to a spouse (I Corinthians 7).

When we hear that it is more blessed to give than to receive, we usually think of giving and receiving money, but it also applies in other areas. If you are lonely or lacking in love, instead of desperately trying to find it—give some friendship, companionship and love. It will come right back to you. There are new people who need a helping hand, older people who need help or those who are in nursing homes, convalescent hospitals or are shut-ins who could benefit from your smile. Many communities have Big Brother and Big Sister programs where you can develop a relationship with a lonely child. Reach out and touch another's life—you'll find love and fulfillment for yourself.

PSYCHOLOGICAL HEALTH

A multitude of excellent books have been written on the subject of psychological health for single people. This section will not attempt to summarize any of them, but rather, present my personal synthesis of practical ideas I have found helpful in a number of areas and some advice on how to get professional help if you feel you need it.

ATTITUDE ADJUSTMENT TIME

Single people may feel that life has been unkind and it may have been. Unfortunately, life has no guarantees for happiness. The happily married couple with the white picket fence may have children in trouble with the law and credit payments they can't meet. No marital situation is a guarantee of bliss.

The Christian is not immune to any of the problems of life, but we do have God's unfailing promise that we are not alone in the problems.

> *"Keep your lives free from the love of money and be content with what you have, because God has said, Never will I leave you; never will I forsake you."*
> (Hebrews 13:5)

> *"And we know that in all things God
> works for the good of those who love him."*
> (Romans 8:28)

"My husband's death broke my heart," said Trudi, the leader of a seminar for newly single women. "But because of his death I was forced to go back to school. I got my degree in counseling. Since then I've been able to work in the women's center here and to help numerous women. You might say that from the tragedy of his death came a new life for me."

Her attitude made all the difference in a tragic situation and so can yours. You have probably heard the little saying, "If life hands you lemons, make lemonade." Well, recognizing that in every life there is sadness and tragedy, my version, says, "Since life will hand you lemons periodically, develop a taste for lemonade." Your attitude is a direct result of the thoughts that occupy your mind. If you think negative, resentful, or destructive thoughts, of course your attitude toward life will be bad. If you think thankful, happy, peaceful thoughts, your attitude toward life will be a joyful one. Not only is this sound psychological advice, but as Christians we are commanded to:

> *Rejoice in the Lord always, I will say it
> again: Rejoice! Let your gentleness be
> evident to all. The Lord is near. Do not be
> anxious about anything, but in everything,
> by prayer and petition, with thanksgiving,
> present your requests to God. And the
> peace of God which transcends all under-
> standing, will guard your hearts and your
> minds in Christ Jesus.*
>
> *Finally, brothers, whatever is true, what-
> ever is noble, whatever is right, whatever
> is pure, whatever is lovely, whatever is*

admirable—if anything is excellent or praiseworthy—think about such things.
                                    Philippians 4:4-8

"I can't help it,"Joyce said, "I keep thinking about the dreadful things John thinks about me and they just aren't true. I've got to make him admit he is wrong."

Have you ever tortured yourself by replaying old arguments, old hurts, old "what ifs"?

Joyce couldn't change John's perceptions during the fifteen years they were married. She doesn't have much more of a chance to do it now that they are divorced. But she continues to play the same torturous mind games. Because of that she isn't making any progress in rebuilding her life now. I shared the verses in Philippians with her and another recent technique I had learned to help control negative thoughts. It's called "thought stopping." Psychologists, following the truth in Philippians, have found that most negative thoughts are not solved by dwelling on them. So when a negative thought enters your mind, inwardly you say to yourself, "STOP," and immediately think about something else. These mind games—and the remedy—also apply if you've just ended a dating relationship on a less than happy note.

I picture the process as something like running on a treadmill. It is so easy to get on the treadmill of negative thoughts. Things like: "Why don't I have more money?" "Why did my husband die so young?" "Why don't people understand how lonely I am?" "Why didn't I do things differently?" These sorts of negative thoughts can go on and on and on settling depression deeper and deeper. To stop them is like deciding to stop running on a treadmill—you get off. You stop the negative thought in your mind and replace it with a positive one.

Some positive thoughts include remembering what

you have to be thankful for. When I was so depressed about starting my life all over as a single person, I thought about the refugees from Southeast Asia. At least I could start over in a country where I knew the language. Remembering verses in the Bible that tell you about God's love and care remind you to pray for help instead of complaining.

In addition to these daily thought changers, there are some larger areas in which a positive change in your thoughts and attitudes can lead you to a happier, more productive life.

GOAL SETTING AND DECISION MAKING

Many women spend the majority of their lives allowing others to make their decisions for them, whether parents, husband or children. This may not have been bad. When you are in a partnership with other people, you work as a unit and take into consideration the needs of others. What is bad is that when you are alone, you may never have had the chance to learn how to set goals or make decisions. Now that you are on your own, these are necessary skills you must develop.

Before you begin to set goals, you have to define your value system. Spend a little time thinking about what is really important to you in life. What is your life based on? My life has always been guided by a little saying on a plaque my grandmother gave me when I was a child. It says, "Only one life 'twill soon be past, only what's done for Christ will last." I've always been aware that the world is temporary, that we are eternal and that our relationship with God is the only thing of lasting value. I have tried, though I haven't always succeeded, to set my goals in light of this.

For example, my priorities have always centered around living for Christ and striving to be conformed to His image. With this as my chief standard, I have something by which to measure my goals and activities. In practical terms this means that it would be rather foolish for me to set the goal of making a lot of money and living in a mansion. Christian writers are not known for their great wealth. A better goal for me is to learn to manage my money wisely. Another goal I have now is to simplify my life in order to have more time for my writing. I love to garden and grow flowers, but a few pretty pots on my patio, rather than a large and complex English garden, is probably a better goal for me in light of what I want to do in my life.

You can see from the examples above that your values not only give your goals a direction, but they also give them limits.

After you have written down your values, write down your major life goals. This would include the areas of family, profession, finances, education, travel, recreation, home, spiritual, relationships and any other areas that are important to you. After you have done this, break down the areas into what you can do to accomplish these goals this year. Then what you can do this month.

A good saying to keep in mind while doing this is, "set your goals in concrete, but your methods in sand." In other words, hold fast to your goals. Always keep them before you. But each month or so look over your methods and be flexible on how you are meeting those goals.

As you work to accomplish your goals, you will need to make some decisions. If someone else has made most of the decisions for you, this can be a difficult skill to learn, but it is essential. "Nobody ever drifted up a mountain," the leader at a women's seminar I attended said. "You have to make decisions on how to get to the top."

Below are some helpful tips on decision making:

1. *It is essential to realize at the beginning that there is no such thing as a* perfect *decision.* You do the best you can with the information you have at the present time. If you make a mistake, remember that mistakes are not bad. It's only bad if you don't learn from the mistakes. In your panic to make a perfect decision and your fear of failure, remember that even if you goof up terribly, just think what a great story it will be to encourage someone else with later.

2. *Always write pro and con lists down on paper.* Writing out the two sides of any decision is very freeing. It gets the battle out of your head and in concrete form in front of you. Sometimes just seeing reasons on paper makes the decision clear. This is particularly useful in making financial decisions. I have wanted to own my own home since I became single. But no matter how I rationalized it in my mind, whenever I honestly worked out the numbers on paper, I realized unhappily that my decision had been made for me. There was simply no way I could afford it.

3. Another helpful thing to write down at this point is the answer to the question, *"What is the worst thing that could happen if I did or didn't make this particular decision?"* We sometimes imagine absolutely ridiculous things that have no basis in reality when we see them on paper.

4. *Evaluate how other people enter into your decision.* Sometimes our decisions do affect others. For example, moving definitely affects where your children will go to school. On the other hand, worrying about what other people will think, or trying to please or impress others needs to be sorted out. Like Ann shared, "I needed to work full-time after my husband died, but I kept thinking

that if I quit my volunteer job at church, people would think I wasn't spiritual anymore. I finally had to realize that what people thought was not going to pay my bills. If I was honestly concerned about serving God and not impressing people, I could do it just as well in a paying job."

5. *After you write things down, literally step away from your decision for awhile.* This is a good time to pray for God's wisdom and guidance. Psychologists have found that in this time away from a troubling decision, the subconscious is constantly working on the problem. At the same time, the Holy Spirit can speak to your heart and mind about the decision. Often, in a few days, seemingly difficult decisions will be resolved and you will know clearly what to do.

HANDLING STRESS

"You know that little chart they have on stress? The one that adds up all these points over difficult things that happen to you and then tells you what your chances are of getting ill in the coming year?" Karen said. "Well, with everything I went through the first six months after my divorce, I should have died about three times."

We laughed, but there is a lot of truth to that chart. Stress can cause all sorts of problems, especially when you are not in good health physically or emotionally. Here are a few hints for handling stress:

1. Realize that stress is a normal part of life. Don't add more stress by thinking that you should never experience stress. One of the biggest causes of stress is the frustration of needs. Realistically, a single woman has

93

many needs, from emotional to monetary, which are often frustrated, so a certain amount of stress is bound to be part of your life.

2. Choose to think constructively. Think of stress as a challenge. Read about successful people who overcame great odds. Walt Disney went bankrupt eight times and wasn't a success until he was over 50. In the same year that Babe Ruth set the world's record for home runs, he also set the world's record for the most strike-outs. Michelangelo didn't paint the Sistine Chapel until he was 81 years old. Bad situations can be opportunities for growth and learning. No matter how bad a situation is, you can learn from it. I can't remember where, but someone told me once to think of life as an adventure to be lived rather than a problem to be solved. I like that.

3. Talk about the things that cause you stress—either to friends or, if need be, to a professional. Talking helps you express the problem and allows you to receive advice on how to manage the problems causing you stress.

4. Learn to be assertive. This doesn't mean being bossy or aggressive or nasty. In its best expression, it is the practice of the Biblical, "speaking the truth in love," (Ephesians 4:15). Being assertive is learning how to state your needs, your desires and your priorities in a positive way. Many women experience stress because they don't know how to say no or are afraid to express themselves.

5. Be sure to take good care of your health by eating and exercising properly. (See previous section on physical health.) Consistent exercise alone has been known to overcome numerous kinds of stress.

6. Avoid self-prescribed medication for stress. There

are many kinds of over-the-counter medications (and alcohol) that can mask the symptoms of stress, but they do not attack the problem. These are not solutions to stress. They will only compound your problems.

7. Balance your work and recreation.

8. If you find your stress comes from fighting other people or things, give in once in awhile. Perfectionism causes great amounts of stress.

9. Learn some relaxation techniques.

10. Set goals. It is tremendously stressful to just float through life with no direction or purpose.

HANDLING EMOTIONS

When we think of emotions, we often think of love and dating and affairs of the heart. However we identify with the word "emotions" most would agree that they relate both to the happiest and most painful areas of emotional health.

Dating is scary whether you're never married, divorced or widowed. Especially today, before you even consider getting into any sort of relationship, you have to decide who you are, what you believe, and what your standards are. You can't allow yourself to get into compromising situations and then try to explain to the other party that you are a Christian and just don't do this or that. Morality and Christian principles are not taken for granted today. As one middle-aged, widowed friend of mine recently said, "the whole sexual revolution took place when I was married. It sure is different today than dating in the fifties!"

Yes, it is. And you have to be prepared for it. If not, even with the best of motives, you can get into bad situations. For example, I have known many Christian singles who, out of loneliness, went to bars to dance and meet people, only to be upset at some of the things that went on there. You have to be realistic. You will not meet fine Christian men in bars; you will not find out if you are compatible with someone by living together, and you certainly won't be living a life worthy of Christ by doing any of these things.

There are many ways for a Christian woman to meet people and to get to know them while doing worthwhile things. I have done a lot of volunteer work at a Christian home for troubled youth. There I met people I later did things with on a social basis. Since we were all Christians, all worked together, and all had the same value system, I didn't have to explain myself to them in social situations. Church groups, volunteer agencies, Bible studies, choirs—there are many ways to meet men and to get to know them in ways that you don't have to feel guilty about. Developing a friendship with someone of the opposite sex first gives you both room to grow.

My sister worked at a church nursery one summer and met the man she later married. There are few better ways to get to know someone well than by watching how he handles forty screaming preschoolers during summer nursery school.

IF YOU ARE ALONE OR
HAVE JUST BROKEN UP

A broken romance hurts. God made us to be with people, to love and care for others. Just as there are people in the world without enough physical food, there are people in our imperfect world without the emotional nourishment they need. There are no explanations;

there are no easy answers. If it happens, here are a few suggestions.

★ Be honest with God. Cry out your heart to Him. Nobody else may understand, but He will. I've written pages and pages in my journal after a break-up that only God could see and always felt better for getting it all out.

★ Ask God to help you learn something from the experience. In another difficult situation, someone once told me, "don't let the pain be wasted." In any hard situation we can learn something.

★ If you have had a series, say five or more, unfortunate relationships, you may want to write down what went wrong with each of them. You may find patterns or destructive traits in yourself that some counseling or therapy may help change. There could be some self-defeating patterns in your own life.

★ Don't dwell on it. Remember your emotions are only one part of your life. Sort of like a stubbed toe, they may be the little hurt part that demands all your attention, but you don't center your whole life around a stubbed toe. Nor should you center your life around shattered emotions. Get on with your work, hobbies, church and friends. Go on a diet—that will give you something to think about. Do some volunteer work for an organization like the people who care for the elderly with Alzheimers disease. It's guaranteed to get your mind off yourself.

LOOKING FOR A PARTNER

We pray for jobs; we pray for our friends; we pray for success financially and in our careers. We recite promises on prayer for all parts of life. Yet somehow we are made to feel like it isn't quite spiritual to honestly pray for a husband.

The Bible says not to worry, but to pray about everything and if you want to be married, it is quite valid to pray for that. In praying, one great guideline comes from Genesis where Eve is described as a "helper suitable" (Genesis 2:18). Pray that God will find you the husband for whom you will be suitable. There are a lot of neat people out there who are simply not suitable for each other. That is one problem of coming to God with a prepared list of exactly what you require in a mate. God knows your heart. He knows what you really need and how you can complete someone else. Praying for a "helper suitable" gives God the freedom to surprise you.

KEEP A JOURNAL

"The two largest problems singles have are loneliness and isolation," said Barbara Bun, senior mental health therapist with the Pikes Peak Mental Health Center. These problems can be especially difficult when you need to talk over a problem with someone, or when you have a special joy or an insight to share. One solution to the absence of a personal confidante is a journal.

A journal isn't just a day by day listing of things that happen, it can include much more.

● Record your feelings and thoughts about the experiences in your life. Describe them in emotional, colorful, dramatic ways you might never express out loud.

● Solutions to problems become clearer once they are down on paper. Use your journal to chart your decision making processes.

● Write down your dreams—both the ones you have sleeping and the dreams you have waking. Look at the patterns and learn about yourself from them.

● A journal is a wonderful place to record insights from reading God's Word and answers to prayer. Write out prayers. Talk to God in your journal. Tell Him how you feel about Him and your walk with Him.

PROFESSIONAL HELP WITH PSYCHOLOGICAL PROBLEMS

"Why is it," Maria asked, "that we don't feel badly if we can't run a three minute mile or climb some mountain, but we feel guilty if we aren't mental superwomen? We don't feel guilty going to the doctor with a broken arm, but when my mental health was falling apart, I felt like I was doing something sinful by asking for help."

It isn't sin or weakness to have problems with your mental health any more than it is a sin to get a cold. At the same time, ignoring psychological problems can be just as bad as ignoring a cold. If you don't take care of yourself, it can develop into something much more serious. Below are some warning signals that should cause you to make an appointment for mental health help for you or a loved one.

1. Does the person act differently than usual? Is it linked to a major change such as a death in the family or a job change?

2. Does the person seem to be withdrawn and depressed? Are hobbies, friends and relatives ignored?

3. Does the person seem to have lost confidence in herself?

4. Does the person complain of extreme anxiety or fear, and does this seem unrelated to actual events?

5. Does the person become aggressive, rude, or abusive over seemingly minor incidents?

6. Is there a sudden change in personal habits such as eating and sleeping, or is the person suddenly noncaring about grooming?

Watch for these danger signs, other problems, or troublesome behavior in you or your children. Many problems in children can be corrected easily with a little professional help but if left untreated can become much worse and scar the child for life.

Even if you don't fit any specific problem area above, but feel intuitively that you need some help, seek it. There are several things you can do to find a good therapist and several things to be aware of:

● As with any other professional, ask for referrals from friends. Different therapists have different specialties and different methods. If you don't like the first one you see, don't be afraid to try another.

● To be sure you share the same value system and that you won't get advice which conflicts with your beliefs and morals, seek a Christian therapist.

● Be aware that when going through a difficult time as a single woman, it may be best to seek a female therapist. Again and again I have seen women who are alone attempt to transfer all their emotions and trust onto an authoritative, strong male therapist. The attendant conflicts are not something any woman needs at this time. Even if this does not happen, it is very hard for a male therapist to really comprehend some of the struggles women go through.

When my marriage broke up, I saw a fine Christian male therapist with my estranged husband. Helpful as the therapist tried to be, he had no understanding of the problems I was experiencing, particularly in the financial area and in the areas that specifically touch a woman's heart. For example, I was having a hard time when I had to sell my home. My rock garden with the little miniature columbines and the mint I'd nurtured for years, the rooms I'd decorated, the curtains I'd made, my *home*—I could hardly bear losing it and I felt foolish for feeling so badly. The male therapist and my estranged husband saw it simply as an economic necessity. When I began to see a woman therapist, in addition to excellent professional counsel, she understood my pain. She told me that as a woman my home was my identity, my heart. She gave me permission to grieve for the loss of that part of me, and she cried with me over my loss.

● In addition to private therapy, there are many groups that are useful. One of the best that I became involved with was a returning-to-work class for women at my local community college. Just talking to other women in my situation was a tremendous encouragement and help to me. Many churches now sponsor groups for singles as well as divorce and grief recovery workshops. Through groups you can learn to express your hurts and needs. You can realize you aren't alone and other people have lived through similar problems. You can also gain valuable objectivity and learn practical solutions.

Additional Recommended Reading:

The Single Experience by Keith Miller and
   Andrea Wells Miller
Growing Through Divorce by Jim Smoke

I will rejoice in God my Creator and celebrate Him!

8

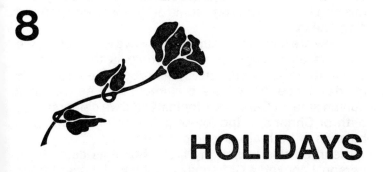

HOLIDAYS

"I've always had this dream that when my birthday came, I'd get all the presents I wanted, that everyone would love me, and my life would be perfect," Amy laughed as she told me this. "I dream that dream every holiday. You'd think some day I'd learn life just isn't like that."

I couldn't laugh too hard when she told me this. I react the same way. There is something about holidays that makes us think life should be perfect during them. I think it has to do with the idealized holiday issues of women's magazines we read all our lives. They never show a messy apartment with a single woman eating a TV dinner to celebrate Christmas. They always show beautiful, huge houses, filled to overflowing with friends and family. The decorations are perfect. The food is perfect, and even the kids are perfect. A little part of our mind always tells us that holidays should be like that. If they aren't, we feel cheated.

103

But reality is that, married or single, no holiday will ever be like that, so don't needlessly torture yourself with impossible, Madison Avenue dreams. Instead, create your own dreams for the holidays. Take a little time to sit down and write out your expectations. If necessary, use this as a time to rearrange some attitudes toward life and singleness.

Below are a variety of suggested ways to celebrate the holidays as a single person. Variety is the important element here. There are numerous sides to every holiday, since many have a spiritual side as well as a human side. At Christmas, for instance, we celebrate the birth of Christ and the joy of giving to one another. A balance in both areas is important.

I learned this lesson my first Christmas as a single person. I cooked a Christmas brunch and dinner for the Dale House, a home for troubled kids where I did volunteer work. I spent a lot of time and effort on it. It was satisfying and I loved doing it. Then I went home alone late that afternoon—and cried my eyes out. I was dead tired and lonely. Later, a friend called and we went out to dinner. I needed both activities. It was good for me to give to others for Christmas, but I had some real human needs for caring and companionship also.

Remember to put balance into your holiday plans.

HOLIDAY CELEBRATION IDEAS

★ Take a trip. This can vary tremendously depending upon your budget. Pretend you're a tourist in your own town. You probably haven't seen half of the things for which your town is known. Take another single girlfriend along and go visit another town close by. If you can afford it, there are cruises and group trips designed especially for singles.

One place to write for cruise information is: Christian Cruise Conferences, 22220 Tulare Street, Fresno, California 93721.

The really adventurous may want to try a do-it-yourself Windjammer Cruise. For information write to P.O. Box 120, Miami Beach, Florida 33119-9983

If you'd rather see the country and drive, there is the American Bed and Breakfast Association, Box 23486, Washington, D.C. 20024 (703) 237-9777 or Christian Bed and Breakfast of America, P.O. Box 388, San Juan Capistrano, California 92693 (714) 496-7050

★ If you can't afford a trip, volunteer to housesit somewhere and in the evening go to a show or movie you've wanted to see for a long time.

★ Go to the special holiday-related services at your church. Try visiting the holiday specials at another church. Consider going on a retreat over the holidays. Make it a special time of prayer and goal setting.

★ Give to people who wouldn't expect it. One of the most innovative ideas I ever read was of a person who goes around giving little gifts to people who have to work on the holidays—people who work at convenience stores and gas stations.

★ Reach out to friends you haven't seen or been in contact with for a long time. Write a long letter with some pictures enclosed.

★ Develop your own traditions. Maybe you can start an annual Easter retreat or a New Year's day open house, potluck, and football game watching time.

★ One large singles group wrote up a calendar and scheduled an open house at different homes for every night between Thanksgiving and New Year's. That way, there was always a place to go and people who cared during a time when loneliness could come or when nothing was planned or for those who simply didn't want to be alone.

★ Call a group of friends and have an impromptu barbecue or potluck at your place.

★ Do something different to your house. Use the time to paint some furniture or a room, wallpaper a wall or do some project you've always wanted to do.

★ Find a friend and go for a hike, horseback riding or any activity you enjoy.

If you want more than just a local hike, try a guided wilderness trek. Outward Bound can be contacted at 384 Field Point Road, Greenwich, Connecticut 06830. Summit Expeditions offers a more Christian focus and can be reached at P.O. Box 521, San Dimas, California 91773.

★ Redecorate yourself. Try a new hairdo, nail polish or makeup. Make yourself something new. Clean out your closets or have your colors done.

★ Instead of eating your way through a holiday, go on an exercise binge. One year during college, my sister and I exercised every day for two hours at a health club during Christmas break. I was so sore I could hardly move at the end of the third day, but by the end of two weeks I was in great shape.

★ Check with your family to see what their plans are. Plan to spend time with them if at all possible.

★ Don't forget to tell God, "thank you." Thank Him for the world He created with times of rest and joy. Celebrate with Him the happiness of being single, the freedom you enjoy and the extra time to do something just for you.

Additional Recommended Reading:

The Holiday Cookbook by Yvonne G. Baker
Creative Hospitality by Marlene D. LeFever

"Lord, I have loved the habitation of thy house, and the place where thine honour dwelleth."

Psalm 26:8, KJV

9

HOUSING

You have many decisions to make as a single woman concerning housing. Will you buy or rent? What sort of home will you live in—townhouse, condo, family home? How will you finance it or take care of it? Do you need or want a roommate? Where do you find one?

EVALUATE YOUR LIFESTYLE

When I was married and only worked part-time, I had time to garden. I loved raising all sorts of flowers and vegetables, and the fun of canning pickles and jams in the fall. When my marriage was over, I had to face the fact that though I loved flowers and gardening as much as ever, I had to make a living. I couldn't take care of a big house with a garden even if I could have afforded one.

As a single woman you have to be realistic about your lifestyle. You may be a widow whose children are grown. You may be a single parent who needs a yard. You may be starting a career that requires relocation in the middle of a city. Or, you may not make enough money yet to afford to buy. Your housing choice must fit your lifestyle *as it is now*.

One caution should be mentioned. If you are newly widowed or divorced and are living in the home you have lived in for many years, do not move too quickly unless forced to by financial considerations. You are going through too much trauma at this time to also contemplate a major move. At the same time, it may make memories a little less painful if you move or dispose of some furniture or redecorate a room.

BEING SINGLE DOESN'T MEAN LIVING ALONE

As a single woman deciding on your housing needs, one of the first things you should decide is whether you want to live alone or if you want a roommate.

Some considerations which affect the decision whether or not to have a roommate are:

★ What can I learn from it? There are many positive reasons for getting a roommate. One of the best is that it teaches you how to get along with someone. No relationship is ever perfect and if you live alone, sometimes its easy to get self-centered without meaning to.

★ Roommates also share expenses, housework and errand running. One of the frustrating things about living alone is that there is no one else to pick up the dry cleaning if you can't. Also, sharing expenses frees up more of your money if you want to splurge on a new dress or dream vacation, or save for the down payment on a new car or a house.

★ Before getting a roommate, realize that having a roommate must be a real commitment if it is to be of benefit. Spend some time being honest with yourself before looking for one. Write down your expectations, house rules, standards on cleanliness, friends and relatives visiting, finances, job and chore sharing, dietary needs, household expenses, et cetera. Have your prospective roommate write hers down also and then together write down your joint house rules. Have weekly or monthly household conferences to discuss how they are working and what changes should be made.

★ Look for a roommate at work or church or through referrals from friends. Take time to get to know the person. It is very important for a long-term compatible relationship to have a roommate who is a Christian and who shares the same values you do.

★ Today, many women delay marriage because of career choices, but at the same time they have the financial resources and the desire for home ownership. Numerous townhouse developments have two master bedroom suites designed for joint ownership. If you and your roommate have gotten along well for awhile, and you are both financially able, you may wish to check into buying something together. In addition to all of your other written understandings, be sure to decide what to do with the purchase should one of you decide to move or marry.

OTHER BASIC CONSIDERATIONS

The next major decision is whether you are going to buy or rent. You may not even have the luxury of that decision since many single women find it difficult to buy. Recent statistics indicate the average home ownership requires an income of at least $30,000 per year and, that the average single woman makes $12,000 a year. Women are finding ways to overcome this difficulty by creative financing, by two women buying together and by various other methods. But you may decide that home ownership is not for you.

In many ways renting is easier for a single woman. You don't have to worry about home repairs, property taxes or exterior house insurance when renting. You are more flexible to job changes, and a sudden drop in salary would not be a disaster. Though there is a tax saving to home ownership, you may still be able to rent more cheaply.

After you decide whether to buy or rent, you then must decide what type of home you want. Today there is a large selection available of single family homes and all sorts of multi-family units that range from apartments to condominiums to townhouses. Again, you need to evaluate your lifestyle and personal needs. If you have children, you need something far different than if you don't. If you can't live without a pet, you have to find a place that will accept one.

If you are considering buying or renting a townhouse or a condominium, there are some additional considerations you should think about.

1. Know the difference between a condominium and a townhouse. In a townhouse the owner owns the title to his residence, the ground under his home to the center of the earth, and everything on his lot including the

common walls to midpoint. A condominium owner on the other hand, buys an individual airspace unit in a multiperson property with an undivided interest in the common elements that bring together the whole—things like hallways and laundry rooms. In very simple terms, townhouses are usually like houses pushed together and condos are like apartments.

2. It is very important to be realistic about how well you get along with other people if you want to try townhouse or condominium living. These housing arrangements are governed by a homeowners group, and whether you buy or rent your unit, you are still responsible to them. Get a copy of their agreement and read through it closely. They may have some rules that you consider strange, and you must abide by them if you decide to move into the units. For example, one development I looked at did not allow you to have your garage door open except to go in and go out. I like to refinish old furniture. To do that in the garage with the door up so I wouldn't suffocate was against the rules. I didn't move into that development.

3. Even if they offer great discounts, think twice about moving into a townhouse or condo development that is under construction. In addition to the noise and inconvenience of construction work, an association needs time to work out the management of the project. You pay a lot for landscaping and other things. Unless that has been taken care of for some time, you really have no idea how well it will be done. Also, some painted exteriors may look great for a year or two, but they can deteriorate quickly. A development that is a few years old and still looks great is a much better long term investment.

One final note for whatever type of home you decide you want. Pay very careful attention to the location. That s the one thing you cannot change. Location is important for your safety, for resale, and for convenience to family, work, friends and church. It needs to be carefully considered.

CONSIDERATIONS WHEN RENTING

"No matter what, my landlord was right there to fix it," said Jenny. "I didn't have to worry about a thing."

"I told my landlord the light switch didn't work," said Amy. "He told me to get one and put it in. 'It isn't hard,' he said! Can you imagine *me* putting in a light switch? I began to wonder what I was paying rent for."

If you decide to rent, choosing the right landlord is just as important as choosing the right place to rent. Talk to the person who will be the landlord. Find out, and get in writing, exactly what he requires of you and what his responsibilities are. At the same time, remember that renting is a business proposition. Your landlord is only your landlord and not a substitute father, husband or brother, so don't expect too much from him.

After you have the right place and landlord, you must have a lease. No matter how much you trust someone, you should have the following items down in writing.

1. All the details of the rent: The exact amount of the rent and the deposit, when the rent is due, and any late penalties.

2. The condition of the rental when you move in and what is expected when you move out. Find out exactly how the landlord defines clean. I have had landlords who were immaculate, and ones who told me a place was clean when I had to scrub grease off the door with steel wool. Be sure you write down any preexisting damage. Find out also how the landlord defines normal wear and tear.

3. Be sure you know how long your lease is for and how much notice you must give if you decide to move. An excellent piece of advice I recently read on renting said to have a clause in the lease that allows you to leave if your life circumstances change greatly. In other words, if an illness in the family or a major job change requires you to move, the normal notice will be waived without penalty.

4. Check on renewability of the lease and what, if any, the rent increases will be. If important, check to see if you can conduct a business from your home. Check on noise restrictions and what the rules are concerning guests. You don't want to find you are forbidden to have guests when your sister comes from California to visit for a week.

CONSIDERATIONS WHEN BUYING

A good real estate agent can be of invaluable help when you decide to purchase a home. He or she can sift through all the legal jargon, help you put together financing, and negotiate when you feel cowardly. Like picking so many other experts, the best place to find a good agent is by asking other single women who have purchased a home. An agent who did a good job for them will probably be able to help you, too.

When you decide to purchase a home, be sure to take a lot of time. A good purchase is one of the best investments you will ever make. A bad one can be one of the worst mistakes of your life.

When you have narrowed it down to a house or two that you really like, take the time and the money to hire a professional building inspector to look over the house.

He can examine the plumbing, electrical wiring, heating and insulation, fireplaces, landscaping, foundations and drainage. Get a detailed report and be sure you understand it. If extensive repairs need to be done, get estimates on them before you agree to buy the house.

Be sure you find out exactly what comes with a house when you buy it. I have known previous owners to take outside plants, light fixtures and other "standard" items that were supposed to stay, but were not specified in the contract. If you assume that the appliances are to stay and find out after you buy the house that they are gone, you could have a big problem. In addition to what stays and what goes, be sure that the seller's promises are in writing and that they are all fulfilled before you close on the house. For example, if the seller agrees to paint or to do some landscaping, make sure it is done before the house is yours.

Remember, anything is negotiable on a house purchase from the amount of commission the real estate agent receives to the financing, from what stays and what goes to the price. Be brave and bargain.

FINANCING

Today you must shop for financing just as carefully as you do for your home. Be very careful here. The thirty year fixed mortgage is no longer the only way to finance a home. Every imaginable kind of financing, both private and public, is available. When you figure out financing, remember that in addition to paying the principal and interest on your loan, your monthly payment will also include taxes and insurance.

Here are a few cautions to be aware of when negotiating for financing.

1. Be sure you completely understand the financing package over the whole life of the mortgage. Some start out with very low payments, but then different things can happen. In some, the payments go up at regular intervals and level off after a certain number of years. Others can fluctuate wildly. Many people lose their homes because they do not understand the worst thing that could happen on some of the variable mortgages.

2. Be careful of the adjustable rate mortgages that fluctuate according to various money rates. These are very risky. Some people who have purchased homes with this type of mortgage have found their payments increasing hundreds of dollars a month. Many financial experts have written extensively against them, and yet recently, when I shopped for a home, the salespeople were talking about how great they were. They gave the best possible example if the economy did this or that. Always assume the economy will do the worst possible and that the interest rates would go as high as possible, then see if you could still make your payments. After all, you will have to make them—not the positive, hopeful salesperson.

3. Be sure your real estate agent fully explains them, but don't be afraid of all forms of creative financing. Some can be quite good. For example, if the owner will help finance a purchase by carrying a second mortgage, or if some private money is offered to finance homes at lower than market rates. There is also the option of "shared equity." This means that an investor can help finance your house, but would then receive part of the profit when it is sold. Be sure to have your lawyer go over the papers carefully for any private financing agreement.

4. Although there are laws against it, the fact remains that no matter what your income, it is sometimes hard for a single woman to get financing approval on a home loan. But there are many loans you can assume without having to qualify in the same way you would for a new, conventional loan. VA loans and some FHA loans fall under this category. They may be a little harder to find, but your real estate agent can help you if you are interested in them.

5. Also, check into the old stand-bys of assuming a loan or having a loan written for a shorter period of time. If you take out a loan for 15 years instead of 30, you will pay much less over the life of the loan.

HOUSE MAINTENANCE

Once you purchase a home, it requires upkeep to maintain your investment and to keep things running smoothly. Some things you will want to do yourself but some will require outside help. Below are a few hints for each situation.

WHAT TO DO YOURSELF

There may not be a lot of actual home repair work that you will want to do yourself, but there are a number of areas with which you should be familiar.

★ First, read all the appliance and maintenance manuals that come with your home. If something goes wrong, you can describe it correctly to a repairman. Also, you'll know when to call a repairman and when to simply change a light bulb.

★ Have all your records accessible. List brands, ages and model numbers of your major appliances such as range, refrigerator, dishwasher, furnace, washer and dryer. If you know these things when you call, the repairman will be sure to come with the correct replacement parts. It is foolish to place a service call for a repairman to come out only to read the numbers off the back of a product and leave again so he can bring the proper part out.

★ Know where your fuse box is and what to do when a fuse is blown. If fuses blow frequently, you have an electrical problem that should be checked on immediately.

★ Know where your water shut-off valves are for each bathroom as well as the whole house. Knowing this simple thing can mean the difference between a minor mess and a major disaster. "I dropped a toothbrush down the toilet as it was flushing," Ann told me. "Something caught somewhere and it began to overflow. If I'd have had to call someone to shut off the water, my carpet throughout the apartment would have been ruined."

★ Know how to light your furnace and water heater. The utilities people will usually come out to do this, but a sudden cold snap can keep them busy for hours. You could get very cold waiting for someone to arrive.

★ Have your furnace and other major appliances maintenanced according to the recommended schedule. Forgetting to change filters and do other routine tasks can cost you hundreds of unnecessary dollars. Have a calendar at home and, along with birthdays and other important dates, write down home maintenance times.

DEALING WITH REPAIRMEN

There will always be tasks, ranging from major to minor, you will either not be able to do or not want to do around the house. You will have to have someone do the work for you. If the home you are in is new, check to see if the problem is under the house or appliance warranty. If so, the company that issued the warranty will send someone out to service it.

For other repair problems, having an all purpose handyman whom you can call is invaluable. Once again, get referrals from other single women. My mom employs a retired man who has unplugged plumbing, cut trees, put in minor woodworking and all sorts of other jobs. He is great. Here are some additional hints for dealing with repair or handymen.

★ Learn all you can about household items such as wiring, plumbing, et cetera. Do this so you will know the proper terms for what you want done. This will help prevent misunderstandings and confusion. It also saves time, and when repair work is done, time means money.

★ If you need major repair or remodeling work done, be sure to get written bids. For major jobs, ask to go see other examples of their work and check them out with the Better Business Bureau. Get a time estimate as well as a cost estimate in writing.

★ Find out exactly what the repairman charges. If it is an hourly rate, decide exactly what you want done before he comes. My mom has a system where she gets all her odd jobs done on a total job rate, not an hourly one. For example, she may need some leaves raked, trees trimmed and a room repainted. She will get a quote for all of the jobs from her handyman. It is almost always cheaper this way, and she knows exactly from the start how much things will cost.

★ When repairmen come to your house, remember you are hiring work done. You do not have to play hostess. Many a woman has found to her surprise that the nice man who sat and had a cup of coffee charged her thirty dollars an hour for his conversation.

★ Don't be intimidated by repairmen and don't be pressured into getting extra work done. If they tell you more things are wrong than you knew about, ask what the options are and tell them you want to think it over. Ask a knowledgeable friend for advice and if it is extensive, expensive work, get a second estimate.

Additional Recommended Reading:

How To Buy Your Home ... And Do It Right by Sue Beck
Sunset Home Repair Handbook by Lane Publishing

Lord, help me to remember that nothing will happen today that you and I can't handle—together.

10

INSURANCE

"If only life were perfect," sighed Jenny. "I could save a lot of money if I didn't have to worry about theft and car accidents. But since it isn't, I bought insurance."

That is why we all buy it. Insurance isn't one of those things we buy because it's fun or we'll look good in it. It's one of those things that fits into the category of a "necessary evil." We must have it to get along in the world today.

On the other hand, insurance isn't protection against every minor as well as major tragedy of life. It is important to find the proper balance in the amount of insurance you have. And few people have that balance. Most people are either dangerously underinsured—including most young single women—or expensively overinsured—a position numerous older single women are in.

Before discussing the various kinds of insurance, it is important to understand the real purpose of insurance.

As Sylvia Porter says, insurance is to protect you from the major tragedies and financial losses in life. In other words, if you should contract cancer, heart trouble, a lengthy hospital stay, or incur a major lawsuit following an auto accident, that is the purpose of insurance. Insurance is not designed to pay the bills every time you need a routine checkup or scratch your car.

Understanding this principle is vitally important when selecting insurance, especially if you are on a limited budget. You can buy insurance for anything and everything—but you will pay dearly for it. On the other hand, you can buy insurance to take care of the major catastrophies of life which would be impossible to take care of on your own. You then budget and save wisely for the little problems that will come along. This means choosing insurance policies with a higher deductible. The deductible is the amount you pay before your insurance pays. By doing this you get a much lower policy cost. In addition, if you pay premium rates for car insurance that covers everything and you report everything, in a year or so you will find your rates have gone up tremendously because of your frequent claims. If you take care of minor fender benders on your own, you will pay lower rates. This does not mean you do not report required accidents to the police. Always obey the law. This principle only means that you don't ask your insurance company to pay for every little thing.

This is only one example of the complexity of the insurance business, but don't let that complexity give you an excuse for avoiding it.

YOUR INSURANCE AGENT

There are two kinds of insurance agents. One kind of agent works for only one company which sells a variety of insurances. For example, one agent may sell auto, health and home insurance. The other kind may be an independent agent and sell various kinds of insurance for several companies. You do not need to get all your insurance from the same company or the same person. I have three agents. One is independent and two work for large national companies. I felt that each was the best one for the particular type of insurance I was purchasing. Here are a few tips to keep in mind when considering insurances.

★ Remember that agents are first of all salespeople. They may present a bewildering array of facts and figures to show you why you should buy a certain type of insurance, but you must be the one to decide.

★ Get referrals from friends as to who good agents are. Get one who plans to make a career out of it and find one who has a good reputation for cooperation in solving claims.

★ Do not allow yourself to be pressured by an agent. A good agent will realize the importance of what you are doing. He or she will answer all your questions and understand your need to take time to check around and think about your decision. Insurance does not have special sales. You can wait a few days before you make a decision. If you feel pressured, get another agent. There are a lot of them in the phone book.

★ Just like agents, all insurance companies are not alike. Be very careful of television, radio and special magazine offers on insurance. If you want to know the stability of an insurance company consult *Best's Insurance Reports*. Your local library should have a copy.

★ Be sure you know the status of your insurance programs at work. What they cover can vary tremendously. Also, find out if your insurance is transferable to private coverage if you leave that company. If you belong to a volunteer or professional organization and have insurance with it, you might wish to check to see if their group rate plus your membership fee is actually cheaper. For example, I could get slightly less expensive health insurance than what I have from a women's networking group to which I used to belong. Then the women's group membership fee went up to around $100.00 a year. Neither the group nor the insurance was a very good buy for me at that rate.

★ A good agent should be willing to sit down with you and go over your entire financial picture. He or she is not being nosy by doing this. You have to have an overall, accurate picture of your income, financial obligations and investments in order to know how to protect them. Again, however, you must decide what to do with this information.

For example, I know that I should have much more life insurance than I do. But right now there is no way I can afford it. I barely have enough to cover my financial obligations and to bury me if I died tomorrow. Since I am self-employed, I also know it would be wise for me to have good disability insurance. But, again, right now I simply can't afford it. For me, I have what I consider the absolute minimum: auto insurance, a major medical health policy, renter's insurance, and a minimum term life insurance policy. These comprise the minimum insurance package any single woman should have. Without them a major disaster could financially cripple you and your family for years to come.

Though it is confusing and expensive, remember there are positive aspects to insurance also. It does give you a peace of mind and protection. So with realistic cautions and hope, let's discuss general guidelines, descriptions and advice for individual types of insurance. Discuss with your agent the specifics of your particular policy, but become familiar with these basic terms below and have a general idea of what the various kinds of insurance are all about before you begin.

AUTOMOTIVE INSURANCE

There are several different parts to automotive insurance. You can get different kinds for different amounts of coverage and with different deductibles. The exact ways in which they apply can vary if you live in a "no fault" insurance state, but the basic definitions will be the same. Ask your agent to explain each part to you carefully.

LIABILITY

In many states this is the minimum insurance required by law for you to have on your car. What this means is that if you are at fault in a major accident, your insurance will pay for the damage to the other car plus medical and legal costs if they are involved. It also usually covers you if someone else drives your car with your permission, and when you drive someone else's car. Since today's costs in this area are rising drastically, it is a good idea to get maximum coverage in this area.

COLLISION

This pays for damages to your car if you hit another car or object and if it was your fault. It will also pay if fault cannot be established or if the other person doesn't have insurance. Collision is essential if you have a new car, but if you have an older car, it is usually not worth it because it will only cover the book value of the car. This is decided by a national standard and does not take into account what your car means to you. It may cost more to have an old car repaired than the car is worth.

COMPREHENSIVE

This pays for a variety of damages resulting from mishaps other than collision. Policies can be rather humorous in this area. They will contain listings of things such as earthquake, lightning, windstorm, larceny, explosion, damage from missiles, falling objects, water, broken glass, malicious mischief, riot or civil commotion, collision with a bird or animal, hail, et cetera. I didn't know so many things could happen to a car until I read my comprehensive clause. On some policies this will also pay for a car rental if you have to have one while yours is being repaired.

UNINSURED MOTORIST

This covers damage to you, your passengers and property when you are involved in an accident where the person at fault has no insurance.

MEDICAL PAYMENTS CLAUSE

This covers medical expenses up to a certain limit for you or your passengers no matter who was at fault in an accident.

MISCELLANEOUS

Different policies have various additional clauses. Some contain extra benefits if you die in an accident or lose a limb.

Be sure you find out about good driver discounts, discounts if you or your children have taken a driver's safety course, or if you are over 65.

If you are a member of an auto club and have free towing through it, be sure you aren't paying extra to have this protection on your auto insurance.

DISABILITY

This insurance is designed to pay a portion of your income if you are unable to work. Not everyone wants or needs it. To find out if you do, think about the following items.

★ What would happen if you were ill for several years while recovering from an automobile accident?

★ What sort of disability coverage do you have from your place of employment, your union or another source?

★ What sort of family resources and responsibilities do you have? For example, do you have children you would have to support? Could you move in with parents or siblings?

★ What continuing financial obligations do you have such as house payments and other big bills?

★ Can you afford it?

If you decide to get disability insurance, here are some factors to consider when looking over policies.

129

★ Is it for illness or accident or both? How does the policy define disability?

★ Be sure it insures you for your particular type of work. Some policies do and some assume that if you can do anything, you are not disabled.

★ Check on time limits. Some start paying immediately but for others there is a long waiting period.

★ Be sure that it is guaranteed renewable and non-cancelable.

LIFE INSURANCE

"Why do I need life insurance?" Joyce asked me when I told her about the small policy I had just purchased.

I replied "Who would pay for your son to finish college? Who would pay to bury you? Who would pay the bills you have if you died tomorrow?"

I could have gone on and on, but she got my basic idea. Single or not, if you have financial or personal obligations that will continue after your death, you need life insurance of some sort. Even a small policy is usually necessary to pay for final expenses because a life insurance policy is paid immediately upon death and does not have to go through lengthy probate proceedings. (See chapter on Death for a fuller explanation.)

Your insurance agent can help you figure out how much insurance you would need, but it is a good idea to have a figure in your own mind first. Remember, you may not be able to afford an ideal amount, so think through this figure carefully. For example, it would be wonderful to have enough insurance to provide for all your children to get through college, but it might be essential that your bills and mortgage be paid off first. To get a general idea of what you need, ask yourself two questions:

1. If I died today, what would be my outstanding financial obligations? This would include funeral and other final costs, outstanding debts, home mortgage, auto payments, loans, charges, college education, income for survivors, and, optionally, any gifts to groups or individuals you may want.

2. List any present assets that you would have to meet these obligations. Do you have a life insurance plan at work? What about other pension and death benefits? What is the value of your present property and investments? What social security benefits would be available to your survivors?

After you come up with a basic figure, decide what kind of life insurance you want. There are two basic types, term and whole life. Some companies have innovative combinations of the two, but these are still the most basic.

TERM INSURANCE

This is the simplest, cheapest type of life insurance. As its name implies, you purchase a policy in which you are covered for a certain term or amount of years, usually five or ten. The face value of the policy stays the same during that time and the premium cost normally increases with your age. With term insurance you accumulate no cash values and the policy automatically terminates at a certain age, usually 65-75.

Be sure your term policy is guaranteed renewable and non-cancelable. Also get one that can be converted to a whole life or other policy if you so desire.

One good strategy for a newly singled woman with many financial obligations, children or both would be to purchase a minimum term policy right away. She should be able to convert it to another kind later or increase the value of it as she is able to afford the premiums. Some women put off any insurance because they can't get an all expenses covered, costly policy, but a $25,000 to $30,000 policy for a fairly young woman is quite inexpensive. Though it would not take care of everything if you have small children, or outstanding debts your family might assume, it could save your survivors from a lot of immediate financial problems if something were to happen to you.

STRAIGHT LIFE OR WHOLE LIFE INSURANCE

This type of insurance combines a savings plan and life insurance. In it, you build up a cash value in addition to the guaranteed amount that will be paid out in event of your death. The positive aspects of this program are that it forces you to save money; you have an investment building, and you can borrow against this if you need it. This type of insurance has been counseled against in most money management programs for the last several years because the rate of return on your investment is very low. Most financial experts recommend term insurance so you can put what you would pay in excess premiums into some kind of investment such as mutual funds.

Because of this, some companies are developing policies that combine the benefits of term and whole life insurance or that offer greater rates of return. Check the individual policies carefully before you choose one of these.

NOTE: If someone dies and you know they had a life insurance policy but you cannot find any record of it, write to: Policy Search Department of the American

Council of Life Insurance, 1850 K St. N.W., Washington, D.C. 20006. They will attempt to locate the policy for you.

HEALTH INSURANCE

"Being without health insurance is like playing Russian roulette," said Linda Ragsdale, head of billing at a major hospital in Colorado. She went on to say that not only should parents be insured, but they must be certain that children also have good policies because dependents tend to be the greatest users of health insurance.

Check where you work to see what kind of health insurance you have, who and what it covers. If you have an excellent plan and it covers all members of your family, you are very fortunate. If you don't have a plan at work, or for some other reason cannot get group insurance, getting medical insurance can be a nightmare.

First of all, it is very expensive. But the cost of even a short hospital stay could run thousands of dollars, so it is essential. Next, the types of policies and the terms can be confusing so take the time to be sure you understand them.

On a private, non-group basis, health insurance usually has two parts. The first is a basic policy that covers limited hospital stays, limited surgery and physicians' fees. In addition to that, you need a major medical policy that would pay for a long illness or lengthy recovery.

Be sure to read policies carefully. The policies that state what dollar amounts they pay are not as good as ones that will pay a percentage or the entire costs because actual dollar amounts are increasing rapidly. For example, a policy might say it pays $50.00 a day for a

133

hospital room. If rooms are costing $120.00 a day, you would be much better off with a policy that says it will pay 80 percent of any room cost. Depending upon your deductible, after a certain amount of expenses to you the major medical will usually pay all remaining expenses.

Be sure you understand the fine print on any health insurance policies. For example, one policy may pay for tests done just before surgery, but if the tests are done more than two days before the surgery, it won't pay for them. Some other areas to check include:

● Know what pre-existing conditions the insurance will not cover and for what amount of time.

● Find out the coverage for nursing home and convalescent or home care.

● Never cancel one policy until you are sure you have been accepted by another.

● Find out if the policy is guaranteed renewable and non-cancelable.

ALTERNATIVES

One alternative to standard health care are HMOs or *health maintenance organizations*. These are usually set up by a hospital, a group of doctors or, as is the case in my town, by a local medical center. These groups are very concerned about preventive medicine. They can be perfect for some people, but they are not the answer to all medical problems. Carefully check all the restrictions for your particular plan. For example, if you travel a lot, find out how you are covered out-of-town. Or, if you have a doctor you like and have used for numerous years, see if you can still use him even if he is not part of the providing group plan.

Additional notes on medical care:

● To keep all medical costs down, practice good preventive medicine. See the chapter on Health.

● For minor emergency care, check into some of the quick care centers that are springing up across the nation. They can be considerably cheaper than a regular doctor if you need a throat culture, a routine check-up or a vaccination.

A final caution about health care should be said concerning policies advertised on TV and in magazines that pay a certain amount per day if you are in the hospital. First of all, these are not health insurance policies. Thirty dollars a day or so hardly covers a fraction of the cost of a hospital stay. Secondly, they are not disability policies. Thirdly, ask yourself these questions if you are considering one of these policies: (1) Since the trend in medicine is toward shorter and shorter hospital stays, and with many operations performed on an outpatient basis, what is the likelihood that this sort of policy would ever be used? (2) Would it be better to spend the money on a disability policy that pays whether one is hospitalized or not, if you want to protect yourself with an income during lengthy illness?

HOMEOWNER'S OR RENTER'S INSURANCE

Both of these types of insurance cover where you live. If you own the home you live in, the insurance covers both the inside contents, the house itself, and the outside of the house. If you are renting, the owner will have insurance on the structure, but this will not cover any of your contents. Many people do not realize this, and find that when a fire or other disaster takes place, they should have had their own renter's insurance. Renter's insurance is fairly inexpensive—don't be without it.

Some basic guidelines should be followed for both kinds of insurance.

1. If you have not had your policy updated in several years, check to see if your policy still covers the present value of your home and its contents.

2. Be sure to get a policy that pays replacement cost of items. All items depreciate, or go down in value, but if they are lost, you would have to buy new ones at today's cost. Replacement value would pay the new, full price.

3. Be sure you know the policy limits for such items as jewelry, silver, musical instruments, antiques, et cetera if you have special collections of these things.

4. Take pictures of the contents of each of your rooms. Take an inventory, and keep receipts and appraisals of valuable items in a safety deposit box. After a fire or other disaster, it is amazing what you may forget and what an insurance agency may question.

5. A good policy in this area will also cover accidents to others while on your premises. For example, if your dog bites someone or they slip on the steps. Check on these provisions.

IF YOU HAVE PROBLEMS

"I got my auto insurance; then had an accident," Georgia told me. "When I went to file my claim, I was told I had no insurance. I panicked."

Fortunately, Georgia's story has a happy ending though the process of getting it was not easy. Her agent had forgotten to file her policy with his home office though he had cashed her check. The policy was sitting in a drawer in his office. The agent was clearly at fault, but he would not admit it. Georgia called the State Insurance Commissioner and filed a complaint. The agent eventually paid for her claim or he would have lost his license.

In my own experience with an insurance problem, I have also found the State Insurance Commissioner's Office to be very helpful. The insurance industry regulates itself through them, and they resolve numerous disputes. Ask an agent with whom you are not having a problem for your local number if you need it.

"I will instruct thee and teach thee in the way which thou shalt go: I will guide thee with mine life."

Psalm 32:8, KJV

11

LEGAL MATTERS

When we think of lawyers, we usually think of big lawsuits or criminal cases. Today, however, in our complex society, we often need lawyers in numerous, more mundane areas including wills, real estate, traffic problems, credit confusion, tenant and landlord disputes. Just as it is a good idea to have a doctor before illness comes, it is also a good idea to have a lawyer before you need one.

Most lawyers do not charge for an initial consultation and this is an excellent way to get to know them. Lawyers are also like doctors in that they tend to specialize in certain areas. Some work only on criminal law; some handle domestic problems; some deal with a variety of cases.

HOW TO FIND A LAWYER

As with anything else, ask around and get referrals. Be sure to find a lawyer who will fit your needs. You probably don't need an expert in criminal law who wouldn't have time to look over real estate leases for you.

Most libraries also have the *Martindale-Hubbell Law Directory*. This directory shows how judges have rated local lawyers and gives a complete educational background of the lawyers listed.

If you don't have personal referrals, your local bar association will usually have a directory listing specialties. Also, many towns have what is called a lawyer referral service. This service will refer you to a lawyer to discuss a specific problem and usually for a very low rate. If the case requires more than half an hour, you may be referred elsewhere or told what the continuing cost would be.

Your phone book will also list low cost legal clinics if your community has them. Although the availability of these has been cut back tremendously in the past several years, they are great if you need legal advice badly and cannot afford it. You do not, however, develop a long term relationship with a lawyer through them.

Pre-paid legal services are another alternative available in some places. They function somewhat like insurance programs. You pay a certain amount and are then entitled to a certain amount of legal advice. Check to see if your work or a professional group you belong to provides this service.

Whatever method you use, choose a lawyer carefully. You must be comfortable around him, able to trust him and to tell him the truth.

ON USING LEGAL SERVICES

Remember that a lawyer's time is valuable. When you

go in to see one, be as organized as you can be ahead of time. Know exactly what you want to find out and exactly what your questions are. Have all of these things written down. If necessary, bring along all important documents. If you are having a will or a contract written, draft it up in your own language first.

When you call for an appointment, always ask exactly how much a certain service will cost and what the payment arrangements will be. Be sure to tell a lawyer that you want copies of all correspondence sent out and it is best to request a draft of it first.

If you are contemplating suing someone, remember that it is not the answer to all problems, and the courts rarely right all wrongs. We see a few spectacular cases reported in the paper, but few people realize the pain, cost and time involved for all parties in a lawsuit. If you are thinking about a lawsuit, first answer the following questions:

1. How have you been hurt? Remember that the courts can only award money. They do not go out and punish the person who wronged you nor show the world how awful he or she was.

2. Even if you win, are you sure the person could pay you anything? If they don't have insurance or large assets, you may win a case but never be able to collect.

3. Can you afford it? Not only in lawyer's costs, but in other fees? The loss of your time and the emotional drain on you and those around you can be extensive. Remember, too, that some courts have up to four year backlogs. Do you want to have your life on hold for that long?

4. Will you have to maintain a relationship with the person you are suing while a court battle continues? This can be especially uncomfortable if the person is your

landlord or employer.

One final caution on lawyers. There is no magic formula guaranteed to provide justice or fairness. Lawyers are only human beings working within a sometimes imperfect legal system. The words, "I'll get a lawyer!" will not always strike terror into the hearts of all concerned, nor make bad people do the right things. Lawyers are not all-wise nor all-powerful. Courts are not always fair and justice on this earth does not always win.

ALTERNATIVES TO THE LEGAL SYSTEM

The legal process by its very nature is a win/lose, right/wrong, black/white situation. Life is not always so clear cut, and part of the problem with litigation is that it tries to force complex situations into right or wrong molds. One alternative many Christian and secular groups are trying is mediation.

MEDIATION: In mediation, the parties involved try to come to an agreement outside of the formal court system. This does not work for criminal cases, but has proven very useful in cases involving fraud, personal injury, landlord problems, divorce, child custody, and adoption.

Mediation tries to work out a solution to a dispute wherein each person emerges from the negotiations with positive gains. The focus of the transaction is cooperation rather than competition and seeks to recognize the needs of everyone concerned.

If you are interested in this type of negotiation for your problems, look in your local phone book for Mediation Services.

SMALL CLAIMS COURT: For cases important to you,

but not big enough to take through the legal system with a lawyer, you might consider Small Claims Court. For example, you can't get your security deposit of $250.00 back from your landlord, or the carpet cleaners tore a big hole in your carpet and won't repair it. These are issues the Small Claims Court can handle.

Small claims courts don't handle all claims though. In the county I live in, claims can't exceed $1,000. The benefits of going to Small Claims Court are that it does not take as much time to get a hearing, and you do not need a lawyer. You can represent yourself.

You can find the Small Claims Court in the phone book under the city or county listings. You will have to fill out certain forms or speak to the clerks there. You will then be given a date for trial before the judge. At the trial date, you and the defendant will appear before the judge and each of you will state your case. In most cases the judge will decide at that time, but you may be asked for more evidence. If so, you must reappear at a later date when the judge will hear the additional facts and then make the decision.

The specifics vary from county to county and state to state, but the basic procedure is similar and very simple.

Additional Recommended Reading:

The People's Court: How to Tell It to the Judge
   by Harvey Liven
Law for the Layman by George Gordon Couglin

"Honour the Lord with thy substance, and with the firstfruits of all thine increase."
Proverbs 3:9, KJV

12

MONEY MANAGEMENT

The love of money may be the root of all evil, but money itself can't be ignored. Pretending that your money matters will take care of themselves will cause more problems than you can imagine.

For the single woman, finances can be one of the most difficult areas to manage effectively. Often others—whether parent or husband—may have managed most of your money for you. They may have also supported you, making for big surprises if you are suddenly alone. As Kay found, newly single women tend to take a drastic drop in income. "I didn't know it cost so much to eat out," she told me. "My husband and I ate out probably 3-5 times a week at relatively inexpensive places. It was relaxing and I enjoyed it. But after my divorce I realized that one of those little dinners would buy me groceries for a week."

Another problem single women have with financial matters is that successful money management takes long term planning. Single people, in general, tend to live in the here and now with money concerns relegated to the time when you will be living with your dream partner in your dream house with its white picket fence. Dreams seldom include how anybody comes up with the down payment for the dream house or how one budgets for upkeep on the picket fence.

A PLAN FOR FINANCIAL HEALTH

If you are a hundred pounds overweight, you know you can't run a marathon next week. If you've never taken care of money or never taken care of it well, if you are seriously in debt or don't know where your paycheck is going, don't expect your financial problems to be solved overnight. But just like a long term diet, if you are consistent and work on things bit by bit, major changes can be made. And, like the feeling at the end of a diet, you'll feel great when you are finally in control of your finances.

Below are six basic steps to get you started on financial health. The following sections will deal with specific areas such as banking, taxes and investments. After going over these, there are two other books that you should read for more information on good money management. They are: *Money Wise* by Mimi Brien, Bantam Books, 1982 and *Sylvia Porter's New Money Book for the 80's* by Sylvia Porter, Avon Books, 1975, 1979.

Before you begin on the following program, set up a financial center for yourself. It does not have to be anything elaborate, but you will need some sort of a desk, a place to file your financial records, a calculator, miscellaneous paper goods such as file folders, and notebooks. Once you have the basic supplies, you can then work out an exact system based on the suggestions below.

STEP ONE: KNOW WHERE YOU ARE FINANCIALLY

This can be painful. Sort of like going to the doctor, sometimes you don't want to know the truth of your situation.

As a widow in her late forties, Jeanie lived off the proceeds of a small insurance policy while she got started in real estate. Used to spending what she wanted, she started to charge clothes, entertainment and various other items thinking that she would pay off her debts when she started selling houses. She didn't sell many right away, but her company gave her advances against future sales. To give herself a lift, Jeanie went to visit her children. Her son lent her a couple thousand dollars. When she got back home, she started to use the cash advances on her Visa and Mastercard accounts for living expenses. By the time Jeanie sat down to figure out her financial situation, she found she was almost $10,000 in debt.

Don't let this happen to you. Be brutally honest and realistic about your finances and spending habits.

Find out right now where you are. Take a piece of paper and list all of your assets: house, car, furniture, any jewelry, collectibles, antiques or other valuables. List any investments that you have. List your salary and any other income you have. It is a good idea to break this list into two parts. In one section list all the assets that you have. But in the other section, list what is available to you each month for living expenses. That is a more realistic figure to work with. You may have antique furniture worth thousands, but it won't help pay the rent next month.

147

Next, list all of your debts, again on two lists. Long term things like your mortgage, if you have one, belong on one list, but you also need a list of how much you spend on monthly debts. Know exactly what payments you have to make and when they are due. Don't forget to plan your savings and giving into this list.

After you have both lists, the most obvious thing is to see if your debts are less than your income. Even if they are, you aren't finished because you need to take the next step.

STEP TWO: KNOW WHERE YOUR MONEY IS GOING

This can be another area of big surprises if you have never kept track of your spending before.

"I never seem to have any money," Cathy told me. "I make a good salary, but I don't have much in savings." So she kept track of what she spent for a few months and it was then easy to see where her money was going. Cathy hated to cook and frequently ate out. She also loved to buy little gifts for her friends. Neither one of these spending habits was any sort of evil, extravagant thing, but combined, they added up to several hundred dollars each month.

To discover your spending patterns, record every purchase you make over $1.00. Get a card or a notebook and take it with you wherever you go. In a few months this will become second nature with you. I have a little card with my calendar that goes everywhere with me. It is divided into categories: groceries, household, clothing, toiletries, eating out, office supplies, medical, giving, and any special expenses for that month like insurance. I also record all basic bills and I have a section for miscellaneous expenditures. Add any additional categories that apply to you. At the end of each month total up each area. By the end of the year you will have a clear record of your spending as well as important totals for costs like insurance, gifts and medical expenses that vary each month.

On this basis you can make monthly evaluations of where your money is going. You can chart the changes month to month; note areas where you think you spend too much; think of ways to do less. "I didn't even think about spending less on food, until I realized how much I had been spending," Cathy said. "Now it's fun to see the total go down each month as I plan good things to cook at home and eat out less frequently."

Your spending habits will also tell you a lot about what is important to you. "After my divorce, for the first few months, I spent money on clothes and cosmetics," Connie said. "I realized later that I felt rejected and ugly and somehow thought I could buy my way out of those feelings."

Money and its management are tricky and emotionally explosive items. You have to realize this before you can begin to budget. Money is more than just numbers on paper. It represents dreams, purchasing power and security. It affects your mental health and social relationships. If you are newly single, the sudden decrease in income can force your lifestyle to be drastically cut. One friend of mine told me she ignored her friends and wouldn't return phone calls after her divorce because she felt too ashamed to tell them she didn't have the money to go out to lunch any more. The decrease in income can be difficult in many areas—especially if you have children and can't spend as much money on them as before. Hard as it is, however, you have to be honest about your situation. As Charles Spurgeon said, "Learn to say no and it will do you more good than being able to speak Latin."

Now that you know where you are financially, and what your basic spending habits are, you will probably want to make some changes.

STEP THREE: REVIEW YOUR RESOURCES

These two areas in your life relate to money, but are not specifically income. The first is people resources.

For help in managing your money, almost everyone needs a good tax accountant, and someone at your bank you can speak to for loans, advice or to simply answer questions. Check to see if your bank has a personal banker program, or simply call customer service and get to know someone in that department.

Then, depending upon your situation, you may also need a good stockbroker and a lawyer. Be very careful of the investment planners that seem to be popular today. If you feel you need one, check to see how they were trained. Be sure they are truly financial planners and not simply salespeople intent on selling you a certain type of insurance or stocks.

Though resource people are invaluable, they are only resources. You should never relinquish your independent financial judgment or responsibility. These people are your advisors. Use them for advice, but learn enough about money management to make your own financial decisions.

In the second category of resources are various things like insurance plans, company benefits, credit union options and all the financial resources to which you have access. For example, a credit union may have a very cheap credit card rate and specials on car financing. Your company may have a pension plan. Some of your insurances may cover the same areas. Check to make sure they don't. All of these are important considerations when making financial plans and decisions.

STEP FOUR: SET SOME FINANCIAL GOALS

Again, you may discover some inner resistance to

setting goals because it is easier to simply go along as you have been, or you may find yourself trapped in the "waiting for a man to come along and make your life better" way of thinking. If you are, tell yourself that when you do find the perfect husband, you'll have a wonderful gift to give to him—a financially stable and wise wife. If you aren't worried about a man coming along, give yourself the terrific gift of financial stability.

Whatever your emotional dreams, set some financial goals. Some may be immediate—to pay off certain bills, for example. Others may be long term, such as setting up an IRA (Individual Retirement Account). Below is a suggested set of financial goals in an order of priority:

1. To know where you are financially each month and to set aside time to evaluate the previous month's spending. This should include balancing your checkbook monthly. It's critical to sound financial footing.
2. To set up a realistic budget and to live by it.
3. To give to God's work consistently.
4. To establish a good credit record in your own name.
5. To have a two to six month emergency fund in savings.
6. To get your insurance policies in order.
7. To buy a house, townhouse or condo.
8. To consider wise, long term investments.
9. To plan for your retirement.

There are numerous other goals you can set, but accomplishing all of the goals above would put you in great financial shape. And while setting big goals, set up little ones, too. For example, I'm saving change in a little pottery pot to get my hair permed. Little goals can be fun—a special dinner or concert, a facial, whatever you would consider too extravagant to normally spend money on can be a treat without guilt if you plan and save for it.

STEP FIVE: LEARN TO BUDGET

It is only with a budget that you can begin to put your goals into practice and make necessary changes in spending habits. To work up a budget, you need to follow the steps below:

1. Know realistically what money you have to spend each month. If you earn a salary where your taxes are taken out for you, this is easy. But if your income fluctuates, or if you get income that is not taxed first, it is easy to overestimate what you have. To avoid disaster, ask your tax accountant for a realistic assessment of your after-tax income. One method some people find useful is to take a predetermined percentage off the top of nontaxed income as soon as they receive it. This amount is put into a savings account until it is time to pay estimated taxes. That way it doesn't sit in a checking account tempting you to spend it.

2. Take out your giving and your savings. No matter where you are financially, plan giving as part of your financial structure. What you decide to give, you give to the Lord. Remember both the poor widow and King David gave of their incomes.

A savings account is very important because the unexpected is part of life. No one is immune to financial troubles, to the loss of a job, to unexpected car repairs, or to extra costs for children. A savings account is not a luxury. It is a method of meeting expenses that you are unable to plan for, but that will one day happen.

A good saying I heard years ago was, "Give 10 percent, save 10 percent, and spend the rest with thankfulness and joy."

3. Plan for your fixed expenses. These include rent or house payments, car payments, phone and utility bills, outstanding charge or other payments, estimated food costs, tuitions, fees, medications, and any other costs

that are about the same each month. Insurance premiums should also be budgeted as part of fixed expenses. One problem many people have with their budgets is that they are unprepared for large, once-a-year expenses such as insurance, a medical check-up, license plate renewals and things like that. To avoid that sudden panic, divide the amount needed for these things by 12 and put aside that amount each month in a special account. It will take you awhile to get this system working, but when it is, big expenses won't be a cause for financial disaster or alarm.

4. Finally, plan your optional spending. For this it might be helpful to have a priority list. For example, if you only have a small amount left over after basic expenses each month, what is more important to you: To get a good book? To see a good movie? Or to have dinner with friends? You are the one who has to decide.

Exactly how you implement your budget is up to you. Some people write out checks for all their bills at one time. Other people literally divide their money into envelopes. Still others have all sorts of automatic withdrawal plans. Whatever method or combination of methods you use, be flexible until you find one that works for you and then stay with it. What is important is that you have a consistent method and that you make the decisions of where your money goes.

STEP SIX: MAKE OUT A RECORDS LIST AND A WILL

No matter how careful you are, if you don't take care of these last two steps, years of careful planning could be wasted. The records list is discussed in detail in the chapter on Organization and the details of why and how to make a will in the chapter on Death.

153

MONEY: BANKING

"You won't believe this," Kay told me one day, "but the department store says you can write checks on an account they have there, and get high interest at the same time!"

Department stores aren't the only places that will offer banking type services in the future. The Depository Institutions Deregulation and Monetary Control Act of 1980 revolutionized the banking industry by removing many restrictions. By 1987, even the controls on how much a bank can pay its depositors in interest will be completely phased out.

The banking industry seems complex enough with credit unions, savings and loans, and brokerage houses all offering various kinds of banking services, but with deregulation this will become even more complicated. Many major department stores already offer numerous financial services, and in the future more will. In theory this will make the banking industry more competitive and flexible.

At the same time, problems have arisen with the new flexibility. People tend to trust any institution that calls itself a bank, but over the past year or two the failures of some of these "banking institutions," show that they are not all the same. The important thing to check on is who insures the deposits at the bank. Institutions insured by both private and state agencies have failed. Unfortunately, some of these institutions pay very high rates of return and many people are attracted to them. Especially if your money is tight, you may be tempted to try to get the highest return you can, but beware of the risk you could be taking. For your money to be as safe as possible, use only an institution insured by the federal government. This means looking for one insured by the FDIC or FSLIC.

WHAT TO LOOK FOR IN A BANK

First, find an institution insured by the federal government. Then, check around and see what various banks charge for their services and what they pay on their savings accounts. If you can belong to a credit union, check it out. They are usually an excellent option. In addition to good rates, they often give lower loan rates and provide their members with additional financial services.

Even for women with limited incomes it is a good idea to have a checking account. Even a small one teaches you how to handle money and you have a record of where you spend your money. This provides useful information for your own financial records as well as for taxes. A checking account helps you establish a credit history, and you develop a relationship with a bank that may be necessary should you ever need a loan.

Be aware, though, that there is a huge variety in types of bank accounts. Checking accounts come with small fees, no fees and some pay interest. Some include free checks, free travelers checks, free money orders and free safety deposit boxes. As a general rule, the more items offered, the more money you must keep in the account. There are also various kinds of savings accounts which pay varying amounts of interest with different withdrawal requirements. Be sure to take some time to check out these different options.

In addition, be sure you understand the various charges your bank imposes. For example, you may pay a monthly charge for your checking account, but are you aware that many banks also charge for each telephone transfer, for savings withdrawals over a certain number each month, and to answer questions on account problems? Some banks charge $10.00 for returned checks and the same amount if you have to stop payment on a check.

Don't find these things out the hard way. My friend Carol did. She didn't want a checking account, so she used her savings account, taking money out and getting money orders to pay bills. She didn't bother to find out that her bank charged $1.00 service charge for every withdrawal over four a month (a common charge). She was astounded one afternoon when she went to make a withdrawal and was told she had no money in her account.

Finally, don't forget that banks are selling a service. You choose where to purchase that service. If you encounter rudeness, lack of help, or simply do not like dealing with the people at a particular banking institution, go elsewhere.

MONEY: CREDIT

"When I got a divorce, my husband canceled all our joint credit cards," Amy told me. "One night I almost ran out of gas and I had no money and no credit cards. There I was praying I'd make it to the grocery store, the one place I could get cash late at night. I decided I had to get some credit in my own name, but it sure wasn't easy."

Getting credit is a lot like trying to get your first job. Nobody wants to hire you until you've had job experience, but you can't get experience until you get a job. In the same way, nobody wants to give you credit until you have a credit history, but you can't get that until someone gives you credit.

Credit buying is a controversial subject. It can be misused, overextended and abused, but it's a fact of life that it is essential in the way our economy functions. If you do not have a credit history, you may never be able to finance a car or purchase a house, two items that one seldom pays for with cash. Emergencies come up, you

156

don't want to take cash when traveling, you often need a credit card to cash a check. For these and numerous other reasons you need to establish credit.

Before giving some suggestions on how to get credit established in your name, a little understanding of how companies and banks look at credit ratings is instructive.

THE CREDIT BUREAU

I used to think these were terrible places that kept everybody's deep, dark secrets and then arbitrarily decreed who got credit and who didn't. I was totally wrong. A credit bureau is simply a business that records your credit history. This includes your identity, employment, how you paid your bills in the past, whatever loans and charge accounts you have had, whether you paid on them, and if you paid on time.

The credit bureau does not rate credit or determine credit. Each institution you apply to has its own system and their standards can vary tremendously. For example, when I was first single and trying to establish my own credit, I applied everywhere just to see who would give me credit and who wouldn't. I got a charge card at Penney's, but Sears turned me down. I got a Mastercard, but couldn't get a Visa.

HOW TO ESTABLISH CREDIT

First, you have to apply for it. Start small. If your town has stores that offer small charge accounts just for the asking, get them. Then apply for gas credit cards and department stores. Finally, get a bank card in your name. If you want to establish loan credit, take out a small loan even if you need someone to co-sign it, and repay it promptly.

157

Some places will give you credit, some won't—all based on the same report, so be persistent. In general, however, the following characteristics are what creditors look for when determining your credit worthiness.

1. Your ability to repay. This includes factors such as the amount of your income, how steady it is, how long you have worked at your job and how much you already owe.

2. Your capital. What do you have in savings and other assets? What can be used as collateral for a loan?

3. Your character. How worthy of trust are you? Do you appear willing to repay?

4. Your credit history. How prompt have you been about paying other credit obligations such as rent, telephone and utility bills? Is your credit record good?

When you want credit or are looking for a loan, ask yourself these questions first. It is not unfair discrimination to deny a loan to a woman who is not working no matter how much she wants or needs it.

CONSUMER CREDIT PROTECTIONS

Getting credit is only half the battle. Understanding it and learning to use it wisely is the other half. To protect you in your use of credit, the federal government has enacted a number of laws concerning credit. Some of the protections you are entitled to are:

1. You have a right to understand how much the credit will cost you. The cost of credit must be expressed in both the finance charge which is a percent, like 18%, and the total dollar amount, which will include interest and any service or carrying charges.

This is a law to protect you. Take advantage of it.

"I just needed the money," Carol told me, "and I didn't really understand the terms of the loan. When I took time to find out, I realized I had paid on it for three years without reducing the principal at all."

Carol's situation is quite common. Just because the truth of what you are paying in interest is frightening, don't hide your head in the sand and pretend it isn't happening.

2. If you have been denied credit, the creditor must notify you in writing within 30 days, and give you either specific reasons for the denial or inform you of your right to request an explanation. If the decision to refuse your loan or credit request is based on information from a credit bureau, the creditor has to tell you the name and address of the agency that supplied the information. The agency is then required to allow you to review your credit file free of charge.

3. You have a right to correct errors on your credit report and to file your side of the story in the credit file of a disputed situation.

4. You can purchase a credit report on yourself at any time. Look up a local credit bureau in the phone book. As you work on getting credit in your own name, be sure correct information is being reported.

MONEY: TAXES

Though you should see your accountant for specific tax questions, these suggestions may help you in this area:

★ Get a good tax accountant, and early in the tax year tell him or her your financial situation. At that time he can suggest deductions you may not have considered and ways for you to keep records of those deductions.

For example, if you do a lot of charity work, are you aware that you can deduct mileage to and from that work? That is one positive benefit it helps to know about early. On the other hand, the laws changed this year and I have to log in daily the amount of time I spend on my word processor, as I use it, or I can't deduct the cost of it from my taxes. That would have presented serious problems if I hadn't found that out until the end of the year.

★ Once you have found out what records you need to keep, keep them. It does not have to be a complex system. A large file folder that holds all your clearly labeled receipts is fine. Once a quarter take them out, put them into categories, and total them.

★ If your financial situation changes drastically during the year, be sure to call your tax advisor to see how this affects you. For example, if you consider buying or selling a house or other property, if you start work or your own company, if you incur a large debt or receive a large amount of money, always call before you make a final financial decision. Tax consequences can be very important.

★ Don't panic if you get a notice that says you made a mistake on your tax returns or that you are going to be audited. My accountant says that the IRS makes mistakes, too. If you are honest and have careful records, your accountant can usually straighten out the problem.

★ If you are separated but not divorced yet, be sure to consult your tax accountant. Changing the date the divorce is final, especially if it is going to fall near the beginning or end of a year, can make a big difference in what both of you will owe in taxes. Your marital status on December 31 is what the IRS will count for the whole year. Only your accountant can tell you which would be the best tax situation for your particular case.

★ If you cannot find copies of your previous tax returns, you can write to the IRS for copies of them. You should be familiar with your past tax situation for proper financial planning in the future.

★ Finally, if your income is small, you own no property, and have no special expenses, you may want to do your own taxes. If you run into problems, call information for the IRS toll-free number.

MONEY: INVESTMENTS

This section can't tell you what specific investments to make. Good investments change with the financial climate from year to year and are dependent on far too many factors to discuss in detail here. The advice below will, however, help you with any investments you decide to make.

There are two major cautions to remember in this area. First, if you have just received a large amount of money, for example the proceeds of an insurance policy, do not make any investments too quickly. Put the money in a secured money market fund at a bank you trust. It will draw a good interest rate and give you time to learn about investments before you make any major decisions. Above all, do not listen to any advice on how to double your money quickly or get rich quick schemes no matter how sophisticated or well meaning they may sound.

Second, investing should not even be considered until your other money management matters are under control. This means you have a workable budget, stable income, adequate savings and a solid base of necessary insurance. Once these areas are all under control, then you can consider investing.

BEFORE YOU CONSIDER INVESTING

Take time to learn about investing. Read the money books recommended elsewhere in this chapter. Read the business and financial section of the newspaper daily. Learn the jargon associated with investing. It is a fascinating world and fun to learn about.

Evaluate your investment personality. Do you like to take risks? Are you the kind of person who can take a loss and never regret it? You have to be if you decide to buy penny stocks. Are you conservative in your investments? Would you rather have a lower rate of return, but be guaranteed that you would always get that return? Some government issues may be best for you. Would you like to do a little of both?

These issues are very important because there is no such thing as the *perfect* investment—one that is totally safe and yields the highest rate of return with no work on your part. Every investment is a combination of trade-offs in the areas explained below. An investment may be good in one area and not so good in another. To decide which investment you want, you have to know which areas are most important to you. The areas you want to understand about any investment are:

1. DEGREE OF RISK. Just as the name implies, this is the variable where your money is either safe and the interest rate is guaranteed or could you lose everything if things do not go well. A super safe investment with little or no risk is your guaranteed savings account at a government insured bank. High risk investments are certain kinds of stocks.

2. LIFESPAN OF THE INVESTMENT. Some investments must be left untouched for a certain number of months or years to achieve the highest rates of return. If your money is taken out before the stated time, you can face a substantial penalty. Certain certificates of deposit

are like this. Others can be taken in and out at any time and the rate of return is not penalized. Most money market funds are in this category.

3. LIQUIDITY. This is how fast you can turn your investment into cash. Real estate is one of the most non-liquid investments. You can't just decide to sell your house tomorrow, and then collect the money. Stocks are very liquid. So are money market funds.

4. TAX IMPACT. The profits on some investments are not taxed, as is the case with certain municipal bonds. This makes their rate of return higher in actuality than the stated rate, depending upon the tax bracket you are in. Some investments have the taxes deferred on them. This is the situation with IRA's. Especially if you are in a higher income tax bracket, be sure to discuss the tax implications of any investment with your accountant.

5. POTENTIAL RETURN. Simply stated, this is how much you might make off the investment. This can vary widely. Some people have made fortunes off the stock market, some have lost fortunes in it. Some have slowly made a good income off more conservative investments whose guaranteed return kept building year after year. We all want to make the highest return, but always remember to balance this figure against other investment factors such as the degree of risk involved in the investment.

6. OWNER INVOLVEMENT. This is how active you must be in your investment. It is true that a fortune can be made in real estate, but you have to spend a tremendous amount of time and energy to do it. You can't find, finance, purchase and sell real estate without spending a lot of time on it, and this does not include doing any fix up or landlord work. That would be extra. On the other hand, you don't have to do anything to make money from certificates of deposit. Again, your personality is an important factor here.

Once you understand each of these factors, the next

most important thing to remember in investing is to diversify. This is the "don't have all your eggs in one basket" principal. No matter how safe or secure your investment seems, it is best to spread your investments around, just in case the impossible and unthinkable happens.

You will need someone to handle your investments for you. Usually this is a stockbroker. Like any other professional, talk to several to find one with whom you are comfortable, who speaks a language you understand, and who is honest. Just like insurance people, stockbrokers are primarily salespeople. You are the one to make all final decisions on your investments. Learn enough about them so you can make them wisely.

Additional Recommended Reading:

From Money Mess to Money Management
   by Patricia H. Rushford

"Great is our Lord, and of great power: his understanding is infinite."
Psalm 147:5, KJV

13

ORGANIZATION

"Being organized means being in control," says Jan Dean, a lady who teaches seminars on "The Well-Organized Woman."

When so much of life seems out of control for a single woman, I find anything that gives back some measure of control very appealing.

This love of control comes from the same motivation that causes me to clean house when I'm really upset. Total chaos is hard to handle. But order, even if it means no dust on the furnitur᷍ is somehow comforting. And I find that when the exterior of my life has some semblance of organization, the interior seems more settled.

Being organized has other benefits. When you are organized you save time. You know where things are. You don't spend needless time looking for important items. You avoid unnecessary panic. Suppose your wallet is stolen. If you have an immediately accessible record of credit card, driver's license and other important numbers and information, you turn a potentially major disaster into an inconvenience.

Jan Dean also says, "Just about the best thing you can do for yourself is to delete unnecessary objects from your life. If you haven't used something in 3-5 years, chances of it coming in handy are pretty slight." She has some cautions on getting organized. "It will take time to get organized, so be prepared for that. It isn't something that you do once and are finished with. It requires constant vigilance to live the clutter-less life." She warns, "For everything you bring into the house you should get rid of something." Finally, she says that if it just kills you to get rid of something, box it up and put it away for 6 months. If you haven't needed it at the end of that time, then toss it.

In a way, this whole book is about organization, about putting the various parts of your life in order so that you will be in control of them.

TIPS ON ORGANIZATION

When you are trying to get organized, find a system that is individually tailored for you. No organizational system is useful if it takes more time to keep the system functional than it saves. To find the system that works for you, take some time and visit the stores (such as office supply stores) that specialize in such items. You'll find an excellent selection of useful items and just visiting the stores will give you lots of ideas.

One of my favorite time organization tips is to handle anything that comes across your desk only once. Paper shuffling, combined with procrastination, is one of the biggest time wasters in anyone's life. One way to solve this is to take a certain amount of time each day to deal with your mail as it arrives. Decide what to do about sales, bills, correspondence, et cetera, at that time. Train yourself to make decisions instead of shuffling papers around on your desk until you drift into a decision.

Another good tip for organizing time is to schedule realistically. Women have many responsibilities and often no one with whom to share them. It is easy to over-schedule and to become frantic. In the same way that I find it very useful to have a junk drawer, so, too, it is a good idea to set aside some time where you never schedule anything. That is your "junk time," time to fit in odds and ends of activities that don't seem to fit in anywhere else, time to relax and not worry about getting more behind on your schedule.

In addition to being a useful practice mentally, cutting down on clutter and useless items seems to benefit one spiritually. Many articles and books have been written on simplifying one's life. Take some time to read one for ideas and inspiration.

ORGANIZING IMPORTANT PAPERS

It is essential that you organize the important papers of your life. To do this you will need three things. First you will need a master list; second you will need some sort of an at-home storage place, and finally, a safety deposit box at your bank.

Your master list will contain basic, important informa-tion and the location of important papers. You should keep one copy of your master list, one should be with a trusted friend and, if you have a personal attorney, that person should have a list also. On the list you should have:

167

1. Your name, address, birthdate, social security number and driver's license number.

2. Name, address and phone number of the following people: parents, best friend, clergyman, children, lawyer, tax accountant, insurance agent, broker, any other people who would have important information concerning your personal or business affairs.

3. The location and number of all bank accounts.

4. The location, information, and agent for all insurance policies.

5. All credit card account numbers.

6. Safety deposit box number and location.

7. A listing of special wishes in case of death, burial plans, et cetera.

8. A list should be kept of the location of the original copies of important items. The items that fall in this category are: birth, marriage and death certificates; adoption and custody papers; citizenship papers; divorce and separation decrees; military papers; property settlement agreements; deeds, titles and mortgage papers; inventory of household possessions; motor vehicle titles and registrations; stocks, bonds and any other important or hard-to-replace papers. A good place for all originals of these items is in a safety deposit box. But since you often need to consult these items in your business decisions, make a xerox copy and keep it at home.

9. The following items should be included on your master list, but they could be kept in a safe place at home: tax returns, medical records, diplomas and transcripts, any other papers that are important, but copies of which could be replaced by the issuing agency.

Additional Recommended Reading:

The Woman's Complete Home Organizer
   by Rena Stronach
Confessions of a Happily Organized Family
   by Deniece Schofield

He is no fool who gives what he cannot keep, to gain what he cannot lose.
Jim Elliott

14

RETIREMENT

They call them "the golden years" and "the best part of life."

Why then is retirement always near the top of the list as one of the greatest causes of stress in life? Why then are so many retired people, especially widows, living at or below the poverty line?

The rosy picture of retirement may be what we dream of, but dreams don't come true just by wishing. Planning, realism, and discipline in the early years of life are what will make retirement a dream come true. Without planning, retirement can be a nightmare.

At no time in history has this been more true. Advances in medicine and general health care have made it a certainty that most of you reading this book will have a far longer retirement than many of our parents ever imagined possible. In addition, you will be healthier, more active and more productive in your reetirement years than any previous generation.

It is never too early or too late to plan for retirement. The earlier you begin to plan and save, the easier it is. But even if you are in your late fifties, it isn't too late to start. No matter what your age, you must assume responsibility for your retirement. Because families are so scattered, it is unrealistic to count on family members to take care of you. Social security, at best, can supply only part of your needs. At the present time, statistics show it will provide about 30-40% of a needed retirement income.

Retirement planning isn't a separate part of life. Many of the other chapters in this book can help with your planning. Many people face a chaotic retirement because they have lived a chaotic life. You need to be organized financially, legally, spiritually and practically through all of life. Taking care of these things through a lifestyle of discipline and giving will make your retirement an extension of your good habits.

As with all other areas, before you decide on specific plans, spend some time thinking through what is important to you in your retirement. Do you want a comfortable house with two guest rooms so your grandchildren can visit often? Do you want to travel and see what you've always read about? Do you envision finally finding time to paint or write poetry? Do you want to try a year as a missionary or Peace Corps volunteer? What standard of living do you need? No two retirement plans will ever be alike, but a definite plan is essential to making your retirement years the "golden years."

To help you formulate your plans and to help you have a happy and productive retirement, think through and begin working on the following areas.

FINANCES: This, of course, is the primary area. If you don't have enough money to live on, it's rather useless to discuss retirement travel or hobbies. First of all, evaluate what assets will be available to you. Do you have a pension plan at work? Widow's benefits? Any inheritances or trusts coming to you?

What are you doing to create a good financial base for your retirement? IRA and Keogh plans provide retirement income in addition to tax savings at the present time. You are never too young to start one. Also, you do not have to contribute the maximum possible to begin one. No matter what amount you start with, you are establishing the habit of planning ahead to finance your retirement. Once the habit is established, you can increase the amount whenever your budget will allow it.

Many women marry later today; many divorced women remarry later in life. What financial obligations do you foresee going into retirement? In neither of these cases can you take it for granted that you will have a house paid for when you reach age 60 or so. Parents are living longer also. What obligations do you have there? A 60-year-old child responsible for a parent in his 80's and who may live close to 100 years of age has to consider the financial obligations they may have. All of these concerns should be thought through in addition to the other items discussed in the chapter on Money Management.

JOB: In thinking about retirement, consider your present job. Is it one that has a mandatory retirement age? Or can you work as long as you are productive and want to work? If your job does enforce required retirement, and if that idea doesn't appeal to you, perhaps you should consider starting a part-time job now that would not require you to stop working. Many people have successful businesses after retirement. Service jobs, sewing, art, writing, sales, and many others are often done successfully by "retired" people.

In addition to the financial aspects of your job, how closely do you identify with it? For example, if you have been a teacher for 40 years, what happens to your self-identity when you are no longer in a classroom? If you look at yourself and see your identity, free time and friends all centered around your job, you may want to broaden your friends and interests before retirement.

HEALTH: One of the largest concerns in retirement is health. No one wants the poor health that is often associated with old age, but most people feel it is inevitable. Many, many studies however, show that good health is possible even at advanced ages. At any age, however, good health requires careful nutrition, exercise and good mental health care. (See the chapter on Health for specific suggestions.) Healthful habits should be integral to all of life.

LEISURE TIME: Do you have hobbies, sports, or other activities that you enjoy, or does work occupy all your time? If you life revolves totally around work, it may not be easy to adjust when you retire.

How do you react to a long vacation? Do you enjoy it or do you wish you were working again? This can be a mini-picture of how retirement may affect you. If you don't like what you see, start developing new interests now.

HOUSING: Most people want to move into smaller, easier-to-care-for homes when they retire. The recent surge in condos and townhouses is a wonderful boon for many retired people. My mother moved into a new townhouse this year and it is a dream come true for her. It is all on one level; all the yard work is done; it is in a safe and secure area. I feel much better knowing she is there.

However, don't move to a new state or a retirement community too quickly. (See the chapter on Housing.) If one appeals to you, make several extended visits to it before you decide to relocate permanently.

SERVICE: Retirement often seems to be equated with an "everything should give me pleasure and entertainment" way of thinking. This often results in bitter older people who feel cheated if they aren't able to travel or have as much "fun" as some of their friends.

The Bible tells us, "it is more blessed (or happier) to give than to receive" (Acts 20:35). That is true for all of life. The happiest retired people I know are people whose lives are still giving to others.

I recently read of two retired nurses who set up a clinic for poor people in South America. I have retired friends who have gone to Africa for a year as missionaries. Many mission boards will place retired people for short term work. The Peace Corps is now actively recruiting retired people and they report a tremendous response by the people in the countries where they are sent. Many cultures value age and experience far more than Americans do. In thinking about retirement, imagine ways you can use the extra time and income to invest your life in service to othes. The word *retire* is never used by the Lord. He always has a place where you are needed.

Additional Recommended Reading:

The Best Half of Your Life by Ray and Anne Ortlund

"The name of the Lord is a strong tower: the righteous runneth into it, and is safe."

Proverbs 18:10, KJV

15

SECURITY

None of us wants to think about being a victim of crime because we think that crime is what happens to other people—not to us. But if we don't think about it, if we don't take steps to protect ourselves, we make it much more likely that we will become a victim. Ray Johnson, a former criminal and now a crime prevention expert, said in a recent magazine interview, "You have to take a good, hard look at the world the way it really is—not as you wish it were. You can't continue to think, 'it couldn't happen to me.' It could."

There is never any guarantee of total personal safety, but there are many things you can do that can significantly reduce your chances of becoming a victim of crime. Each section below will give you several ideas.

HOME SAFETY

Psychological tricks are one of the best ways to protect your home. This means that a home is much less likely to be broken into if burglars think someone is home. Do all that you can to give that impression.

★ Some surveys say that the silver toned tape used to wire windows for burglar alarms is nearly as effective a deterrent as a fully operational alarm system.

★ Whether home or away, if you leave a bathroom light on and the door slightly ajar, it gives the appearance of someone in the bathroom about to come out—a situation no burglar wants.

★ If your neighborhood doesn't have a neighborhood watch group, contact them and see if you can get one started. They have been very successful in cutting down crime in the communities that use them. Police will come out and give you tips and procedures for preventing crime. This can work especially well in ready made communities such as townhouse and condominium developments.

Check to see if your police department will come out and make a security survey of your home and suggest crime prevention techniques. Some do.

Also, most large police departments offer the free use of a special marking device with which you can etch your Social Security number into any item likely to be stolen. This allows it to be easily traced and returned to you in the event of theft.

★ Be sure you have effective window and door locks and keep them locked. Studies show that in over half the household burglaries, the burglar usually entered without force, most frequently through an unlocked door or window, sometimes by using a key. A door chain is not an adequate lock. They are easily broken. While checking on locks, be sure to check the putty in your windows. If it is old and crumbling, a burglar could just push the window through.

★ Consider getting a dog. Even a small one makes noise at unfamiliar people approaching, and noise is one of the great deterrents to crime.

★ Never open your door to a stranger. If someone says they have a problem such as car trouble, make a phone call for them. Never allow a repairman or someone in a uniform to come in unless you know or were expecting him. Any uniform can be stolen or rented.

★ If you come home and sense you have been broken into, do not go into your house. Go to your neighbor and call the police. If you are home and you hear something, avoid contact with the burglar at all costs. One bluffing technique that has been suggested is to yell at the top of your voice, "George, there is a burglar downstairs!"

HOME SAFETY PRECAUTIONS WHEN YOU HAVE TO BE AWAY

★ Have automatic timers set to turn lights and the TV on and off at certain times.

★ Either take the phone off the hook or use a telephone answering machine. If you use an answering machine, make sure the message says you can't come to the phone rather than one that tells everyone how long you will be away from home.

★ Do not cancel your mail and newspapers, but have a friend pick them up daily. One does not want to be overly suspicious, but you never know what sort of friends your paperboy might tell that you are going to be out of town for a week.

179

★ When getting ready to go on a trip, load your bags into the car in the garage. Don't advertise that you are leaving to chance passersby.

★ If a friend has a second car, or if you aren't taking yours, park it in the driveway while you are gone. Not only does it look like someone is home, but a burglar cannot pull up close to a house if a car is parked like that.

★ One of the best ways to protect your home when you travel is to have a housesitter. Check with the college age class at your church or a similar group. You will probably be able to find someone who would enjoy staying in your home for the price of a well-stocked refrigerator.

CAR SAFETY

Eighty-five percent of the crimes that occur away from home occur in or around your car, so follow these tips for safety.

★ Always have the key to unlock your car door in your hand before leaving a building enroute to your car. Be aware of your surroundings as you walk to it.

★ If you shop at night, always have someone help you out to your car with your groceries or packages. If approaching your car alone, check around and under it.

★ This is seldom recommended in crime prevention tips, but I think one of the best security factors for car safety is my dog. I always take him with me when going to a strange place or driving at night. I don't worry about coming back to my car, or someone trying to break in when he is in it.

★ Never drive with your gas tank close to empty. If you

should have problems, have a sign in your car that you put in your window that says, SEND HELP. If anyone stops, do not get out of your car and do not accept a ride from anyone. Ask them to call the police or your auto club for help. Stay with your car until help arrives. Keep the phone number of a trusted friend on a sheet of paper that you can show through the car window and ask the person to call them.

★ If you are about to be attacked when near your car but not in it, you can always yell and run toward lights and people. Or, you can scream your head off and roll under your car. Few muggers will try to pull you out. If someone tries to attack you while you are in your car, lay on the horn. You can also ram the car in front of or in back of you. If you are driving and feel you are being followed, drive to the nearest police station or well lit gas station. Never drive home.

★ If someone bumps your car and you are alone, or it is a suspicious looking person, don't get out to exchange information. Memorize or write down the license number, then drive straight to the police station and report it.

★ No matter who it seems to be, if you see someone waiting in your car, do not approach. Go back to where you were and get a security guard or call the police.

VOIDING RAPE

One third of all rapes occur in the victim's home. So practice the home safety tips above and these suggestions, too.

★ If you are in an unavoidable situation and must walk alone through an undesirable neighborhood or after dark, walk confidently and think mean.

★ Be sensible. Do not jog or walk alone, especially at night. Don't use apartment or public laundromats late at night. Don't use rear stairwells. Don't live where you have to park a long way from your door.

★ There are a number of self-defense classes for women. Some experts recommend them, some advise against them. One good piece of advice I heard is that they do give a woman a choice. You have to know yourself to know if you would use them and would benefit from this type of class.

★ Much has been written recently about "date rape," or rape that occurs in a social situation when the victim knows and trusts her attacker. To avoid this, never accept a date from a stranger. To get to know someone you may have met at work or at a class, take your own car and drive yourself to meet him for coffee or a dinner or whatever. It may sound terribly Victorian, but do not go to a man's apartment alone, even for afternoon coffee unless you know him well.

★ If you have been a rape victim, call a rape crisis center immediately, the police, and a female friend. Do not destroy any evidence. Do not bathe, douche or wash yourself. Get to a hospital as soon as possible. If this has happened to you and you did not report it, for your future peace of mind, you might consider counseling even now.

SAFETY WHILE TRAVELING

★ When you make hotel reservations with your travel agent, ask to have a second floor room. They are harder to break into than a first floor room. Also, request a room by the elevator. They are harder to break into than a room that is down the hall and around a dark corner.

★ So you don't have to get out your wallet every time you want to give a tip, have a special coin purse filled with quarters and dollar bills.

★ Immediately check to make sure your room phone is working when you enter your room. Never open your door to anyone who says they were sent to check on something or to do repairs. Tell them you were not informed of this and then call hotel security immediately.

★ For additional security when you travel, take a portable smoke alarm and a flashlight. Be sure you know where emergency exits and the fire escapes are. To make your door secure, a rubber door stop works well and so do the shriek alarms that you can attach to a door. They go off if someone touches the door on the other side.

TO AVOID GETTING MUGGED

★ Don't go alone into questionable areas.
★ Don't flaunt expensive jewelry, or clothing.
★ Carry your purse securely under your arm and hold on to it.

★ Follow all other safety information above, and use common sense about areas to avoid.

★ If you are mugged or assaulted, do these things:
1) Stay calm.
2) Don't argue. Give the mugger your money or purse slowly. Don't do anything in jerky or sudden movements.
3) After you have given him what he wants, don't try any heroics. Wait for him to leave and then contact the police.

POSTAL AND CONSUMER CRIME

Crime seems to be everywhere today. If you do everything you can to avoid burglars, drive only in the daytime, never go out alone, and are, in short, careful to the point of being almost paranoid, you still may not be free from crime. Crime can literally come knocking on your door or arrive in your mail. What makes this sort of crime so pernicious is that our first inclination is to believe people. We want to believe we can make money at home stuffing envelopes—the ad said we could. We want to believe the nice man will build us a fence for that fantastic price—after all, he had pictures of other jobs he did. But no matter what we want to believe, year after year, hundreds of trusting individuals are robbed of thousands of dollars through consumer and mail fraud. As hard as it is to believe, hundreds of people each year make their living by trying to defraud others.

Here are some tips to avoid being victimized in these areas:

1. Mail fraud usually occurs in two ways. The first is where a costly product is advertised through the mail but does not do what it is advertised to do. Examples of this include the numerous arthritis cures, ways to lose weight without dieting, or how to become twenty years younger overnight. These products do about as much good as the snake oil the old medicine men used to sell. The saying that "if something seems to be too good to be true, it probably is," should be remembered in these cases.

Mail fraud is also rampant in the work-at-home schemes. This is where you either stuff envelopes or make things. After responding to the initial ad, they usually ask you to give them a certain amount of money before you can learn more about their scheme. Be very suspicious of anything that says you will make a lot o

184

money with little or no work. If that were true, everyone would be doing it. You can no more make money without working than you can lose weight without dieting and exercising.

2. Consumer fraud is most prevalent in schemes that ask for a certain amount of money for a service in advance. Examples of this are lawn work, resurfacing your driveway, building a fence, roofing your house. The con artists will come around, offer you an excellent deal, and explain that they need an advance to purchase materials for the job. It sounds reasonable; the price is right, and after all, you sign a contract. So you give them money and never hear from them again. This scheme happens again and again and single women are often victims of it. Always contact your Better Business Bureau for references before having any kind of home improvement work done, and do not prepay for work.

Miscellaneous other schemes to be aware of are:

3. Never give out any financial information over the phone, no matter who the person says they are. For example, never give out a credit card number. Numerous scams have sprung up lately where someone is called and told they have won a contest or their credit is being checked or some sort of similar thing. The conman says he needs a credit card number to verify something. He gets your number and with it can go and charge hundreds of dollars worth of goods before you find out what happened.

4. Chain letters for anything are illegal and they do not work. Throw them in the trash immediately.

5. Never buy land or any real estate property without personally inspecting it. The lovely pictures you may be shown could have been taken any place.

Additional Recommended Reading:

Home Security Time Life Books

Thou hast made us for thyself, oh Lord, and our hearts are restless until they rest in thee.

Augustine

Conclusion

Restless, often an appropriate term to describe the single life. Restless because of the uncertainties, the loneliness, the fears, the feeling that your life is on hold, all are part of being single.

We feel emptiness in our hearts and we think it is for material security, or for a person. But what do we do when we get those things and the loneliness is still there? What do you do if you follow every bit of advice in this book, and you still can't sleep at night because of a gnawing pain inside? What if you find the person of your dreams? He's everything you've ever wanted and still you're lonely?

I think we misunderstand the emptiness because we look for the wrong things to erase it. No person, no program, no book or plan will ever take away the empty place that only God can fill. He made the loneliness inside us to call us to Himself, but we try to fill it with everything else.

It is good to put the exterior of life in order, but you must realize that when that is taken care of, the ultimately important thing in life is the relationship between you and God. He is the only one who can understand the depth of your fears and the expanses of your dreams. He is the only security, the only one worthy of ultimate trust. He won't leave you in the depths of your depression, in the boredom of your daily tasks or in the heights of your hope. Finally, He is the only one who will not let go of your hand when you cross that ultimately lonely path from death to eternal life.

To know Christ as the foundational truth of your life, and to rest in your relationship with Him is to be the truly successfully single woman God created you to be.